*Cultural Consumer Church... or
Biblical Building Blocks?*

Spiritual Architecture

• A TIMELESS FOUNDATION FOR THE PEOPLE OF GOD •

ROD HOLMES

Ark House Press
arkhousepress.com

© 2023 Rod Holmes

All rights reserved. Apart from any fair dealing for the purpose of study, research, criticism, or review, as permitted under the Copyright Act, no part may be reproduced by any process without written permission.

Unless otherwise stated, all Scriptures are taken from the New International Translation (Holy Bible. Copyright© 1996, 2004, 2007, 2013 by Tyndale House Foundation. Used by permission of Tyndale House Publishers Inc., Carol Stream, Illinois 60188. All rights reserved.)

Some names and identifying details have been changed to protect the privacy of individuals.

Cataloguing in Publication Data:
Title: Spiritual Architecture
ISBN: 9780645802542 (pbk)
Subjects: REL006070 [RELIGION / Biblical Commentary / New Testament / General];
REL006710 [RELIGION / Biblical Studies / New Testament / Jesus, the Gospels & Acts];
REL108000 [RELIGION / Christian Church / General
Other Authors/Contributors: Holmes, Rod

Design by initiateagency.com

Contents

1. The Body Triplet 1
   The Church is a connected body
   PAUL, SILAS & TIMOTHY

2. The Inner Core Triplet 12
   The Church has a strong core
   FAITH, LOVE AND HOPE
   WORK, LABOUR, ENDURANCE

3. The Power Triplet 24
   The Church is powerful
   POWER, SPIRIT, CONVICTION

4. The Worship Triplet 41
   The Church worships the living and True God
   TURN, SERVE, WAIT

5. The TWO False Motive Triplets 51
   The Church gets its approval from God alone
   ERROR, IMPURITY, TRICKERY &
   FLATTERY, GREED COVERING, PRAISE SEEKING

6. The Family Triplet 64
   The Church is a family
   Part 1 CHILD, MOTHER, FATHER
   Part 2 ENCOURAGE, COMFORT, WARN

7. The Intercessory Triplet 79
   The Church never stops its intercessory work
   WAYMAKER, LOVE CREATOR,
   HEART STRENGTHENER

8. The Purity Triplet 92
   The Church is an Exclusive lover
   AVOID IMPURITY, SHOW SELF CONTROL,
   DON'T TAKE ADVANTAGE

9. The Second Coming Triplet 109
   The Church is complete at the last trumpet blast
   REVEALED, RESURRECTED, REUNITED

10. The day of the Lord Triplet 126
    The church is a warning beacon to the world
    NO WARNING: LIKE A THIEF IN THE NIGHT
    NO WORRIES: DURING A TIME OF SECURITY
    NO ESCAPE: IMPOSSIBLE TO RUN FROM.

11. The Children of the Daylight Triplet 142
    The Church is ablaze with light.
    AWAKE, SOBER, INVOLVED

12. The Will of God Triplet 156
    The Church joyfully does the will of God
    REJOICE, PRAY, GIVE THANKS

13. Body, Soul and Spirit Triplet 175
    The Church is holistic
    SPIRIT, SOUL, BODY

Preface

The writing of this book came as something of a surprise to me. We had recently been appointed to a new church in Perth and one of the first sermon series I felt led to share was on 1 Thessalonians. I had always been intrigued by the grouping of ideas in distinct blocks of three that appear in the letter so decided to use them as a basis for each of the sermons preached. The powerful ministry of this Macedonian church that was so well known even beyond their local area pointed to the work of the Spirit in their midst and that started me on this journey. As the series progressed it became quite clear that each of the "triplets of thought" represented a dimension of the church that was very important for us all to grasp. Some of these truths have been sadly lost at times in the pursuit of a pragmatic approach to church advancement. Interestingly enough it was not until I had finished the series that the structure of this book began to form. Once I began to see the actual biblical building block that each triplet represented it became an exciting task to package each sermon in a written format suitable for a book. The overall goal of what has been written is to point us in a direction that all cultures and ethnic groups can use as the foundation for a healthy church. The belief that the word of God truly gives us all we need for whatever we are called to do is the underlying bedrock of this offering to the Lord.

Rod Holmes
Perth, WA.

1

The Body Triplet

The Church is a connected body
PAUL, SILAS & TIMOTHY

"**Paul and Silas and Timothy**, to the church of the Thessalonians in God the Father and the Lord Jesus Christ: Grace to you and peace."
1 Thessalonians 1:1

It is very tempting to think of "the great apostle Paul" as some sort of a maverick blazing through the Roman Empire planting churches on his own and rushing off with the Lord not needing human fellowship like the rest of us! I remember quite distinctly an old advertisement for "Solo" the lemon fizzy drink. A tough guy rests his kayak on the top of a cliff ledge looking way below at a river in the valley. He pops a "Solo" can in his gear and leaps off the edge navigating rocks and trees and all sorts of barriers as the kayak slides its way downwards and hits the water with ease. He then "cracks the can" revealing that he truly is a "Solo" man. This picture of individual accomplishment is not what we see in the life of Paul if we look closely. We rapidly discover he was a strong team player as he truly believed that the church is a body with many members who all need each other. We are all stronger as a result of knowing this body principle. His whole ministry was about planting churches not just saving individuals. He was a powerful evangelist yet evangelism outside of a church planting context would have been very foreign to Paul. His desire to establish leadership and implement healthy structures was paramount in his thinking as opposed to just being a "fly by night evangelist." Within this structure and leadership was always a highly relational approach that led to a deep bond of affection. Leadership for Paul was a union of hearts which is ultimately a spiritual thing and that can sometimes be missing in today's church leadership training and practice. If it isn't missing in theory it can at least be undervalued and down played in the coalface of ministry.

The idea of just hoping a church will develop in a healthy way with no assistance and input was against the whole concept of the body that was planted deeply in Paul's heart. Such a strong commitment to the body arose out of his God given model of the church as a family in which all members are distinct, gifted and valued. His letters, personal visits and constant prayers came out of a heart connection that emanated from the heart of Christ. Paul could not just leave a church to their own devices therefore he did all he could to mature the body of Christ.

Saul who became Paul didn't go alone on the first missionary journey although he had learnt how to be alone with Christ and not need the approval and support of the other church leaders. He had come to that place where he only lived for the approval of God and refused to live out of the fear of man no matter how important they seemed to be in the church structure. This was actually very different to just being plain "anti-authority" as can be the tendency in some quarters. It was a respectful "God fearing" position that invited others to seek the will of God before all other things. The clear leading from the Spirit was to go in tandem with Barnabas and work together as they obediently followed the Spirit to share the power of the gospel in the Roman empire.

They as a small triplet team were appointed at Antioch and then sent off with the full backing of the church. We are told that John Mark came as their helper though he seems to have "caved in under pressure" and went back home …or even "ran back to Mummy" as some might (perhaps unfairly) describe his response. As God is always seeking to redeem us though there was much more to his story! I am so grateful that one failure doesn't lead to an exclusion from being able to serve in the kingdom of God. This initial triplet team was very short lived yet nevertheless pointed toward the need to establish a unit, not just be a solitary operation.

The reduced tandem team did a circular trip in which a church was planted in each town they visited. We then read that they appointed leaders (Elders) in the newly planted churches just a few weeks later on the way back home. When you think about that it can be quite confronting when we are conditioned to choosing leaders after a lengthy process and maybe even spending much time writing and modifying position profiles! Is it possible that we are supposed to be led to choose a leader by the Spirit and subsequently modify the job description around their gifting and personality and strengths? Could it be that others in the body will rise up to "fill in the gaps" and demonstrate that no one person or even small band need "have it all?" The Elders were appointed to lead others into ministry and service by teaching and wisdom. They were also called to be good listeners who were able to ascertain what the Spirit was saying through others to the whole of the body.

Some time later Paul sensed the need to check up on the churches that had been planted. Just how strong were their roots and had they begun to branch out and maybe even produce some fruit? His heart was for the body of Christ to become strong and he was acutely aware what can arise to cause churches to stall, grow in a twisted direction or even fracture. It wasn't a supervisory type of check up from a high position but instead a healthy apprehension that somehow Satan had infiltrated this new work and began his divisive, doubt producing and slanderous work. There is a diabolical enemy of our souls who targets churches and having studied us intently knows our weak points and exploits them. Paul was "...not ignorant of his schemes."[1]

Barnabas wanted to take John Mark and "give him another go." This is an idea that Aussies at least would consider quite important. Paul felt it was unwise though as the pressures of frontline cross-cultural ministry would be too great. Given the different nature of frontline evangelism to supporting an established church we would be unwise to suggest that Paul somehow got this one wrong. When we trained to go to Bolivia in 1993 as missionaries this was stressed quite strongly as too many missionaries experience severe shock of various kinds that short circuit their ministry to a particular people area. Later developments bear out that in fact they were both right in their own way as their "different gifts" and role in the body came to the fore. In other words serious disagreement is not too messy a tangle for the Holy Spirit and may well have elements of truth in both aspects. Barnabas (Joseph who was a Levite) took John Mark and sailed for Cyprus where he came from and encouraged him deeply and restored him to the point where Paul asks for him later in his ministry. Barnabas expressed his commitment to "team ministry" through his gifting as "the son of encouragement." Barnabas knew who he was and was true to his gifting and inner motivations. Paul linked up with Silas (Silvanus) and was commended by the brothers to go and strengthen the churches knowing that Silas would handle the rigours of such a robust and dangerous ministry. Once again we discover that Paul was not a "solo" man. He knew the importance of being in unity with at least one other fellow missional believer. He too expressed his com-

---

[1] 2 Corinthians 2:9-11

9My purpose in writing you was to see if you would stand the test and be obedient in everything. 10If you forgive anyone, I also forgive him. And if I have forgiven anything, I have forgiven it in the presence of Christ for your sake, 11in order that Satan should not outwit us. For we are not unaware of his schemes.

mitment to team ministry through his missionary gifting and unique calling.

Paul and Silas then went on the second journey **picking up Timothy** on the way. His background and temperament brought an extra element to the team. The team was large enough to be able to share the load with their diverse gift mix and small enough to quickly respond to difficulties and move on with minimal preparation. This new triplet team worked together in many settings producing much fruit for the kingdom.

Vision of the man of Macedonia

"...Come over to Macedonia and help us..." Acts 16:9

In Philippi the leading city of Macedonia, Lydia was at a prayer meeting by the river, heard the gospel, was saved and was baptised. Paul then cast out a spirit of divination from a slave girl which resulted in his being thrown into prison along with Silas. Paul and Silas were now incarcerated and flogged in Philippi together yet were living a life of supernatural faith which showed expression by their amazing "rejoicing" in the Lord. Timothy somehow escaped prison yet remained intimately part of the trio. After their miraculous release and conversion of the jailer and his family Paul moves on.

In Thessalonica (Modern Thessaloniki)

Paul and Silas then proceeded to Thessalonica (Θεσσαλονίκη), with Timothy remaining connected. The fact that Timothy has his name at the beginning of the letter to the Thessalonians probably indicates some sort of a relationship and presumably he had met and even connected for at least a short period of time. Paul preached over 3 Sabbaths days in the synagogue so we could say he was there for at least 15-20 days.

Those saved are described as being;

Some Jews
A large number of God fearing Greeks
Not a few prominent women

Acts 17:5 says "...But the Jews were jealous."

They did the following;

Rounded up some bad characters
Formed a mob
Started a riot
Falsely accused them before the city officials

At night the brothers sent Paul and Silas away to Berea.
We then read that the Bereans "were of more noble character than the Thessalonians." They searched the Scriptures to see if what they were saying was true. Those saved were described similarly as being;

Many of the Jews
A number of prominent Greek Women
Many Greek men

But the Thessalonian Jews got wind of what was happening;

They went to Berea
Agitated the crowds
Stirred them up

Paul was sent without the other two to the coast and then on to Athens. Silas and Timothy were beckoned by Paul to join him as soon as they could. This was not because Paul could not handle solitude but because of his belief that a close knit group of believers with the same vision of reaching the lost in an area is greatly blessed by Christ. He believed in friendship in the context of fellowship and shared ministry and valued their presence, input and closeness.

Later on Paul also visited Thessalonica and Berea on his third missionary journey. In all of this in so many ways we see the Apostle Paul always seeking fellowship, building churches, facilitating team ministry and refusing to go it on his own unless it was a real emergency. How important it is to be part of a body, a family, a team. In the last part of the Lord's prayer it says or shall we say Jesus prays….

"deliver us from evil."[2]

The pronoun is not first person instead it is deliver "us." This indicates a corporate approach, a team, a body, a family. In other words our life as a believer is not supposed to be lived separated from our local church family.

Don't try and do it alone

It is an old adage in nature that the mob or herd are safer together. When a lone animal tries to manage on their own they rapidly succumb to the attacks of the predators who work as a group to bring the weak stragglers or reckless adventurers down. Too often a lone Christian tries to keep on following Christ and with considerable effort attempt to remain faithful, holy and true. All too quickly though we can become "easy pickings" and be torn to pieces by the wolves.

Jesus designed the church to be a body, a family, a flock. This design was intended for our protection and growth and because we are created as deeply relational beings. Jesus Christ does not call us into individualism even though our faith must be personal, true and authentic. Our faith ultimately must not be borrowed from another person though they

---

[2] And lead us not into temptation, but deliver us from evil: For thine is the kingdom, and the power, and the glory, for ever. Amen. Matthew 6:13 KJV

may have been our mentor or teacher. **This holy tension of individual obedience and corporate functioning must be constantly maintained.**

Paul did go away on his own for a while but what we discover of this fiery disciple is his deep heart for people and his courage to work through all the problems. He didn't just say I'm not into church politics as so many say nowadays. Unfortunately this can mean *"I don't like being with the living stones that the master builder has placed around me in the edifice which is the living temple of Christ, his body, the church."* Paul courageously jumped into tough situations out of love for Christ and his body no matter how stormy it got and it did become very rugged for him at times. He was frequently spoken against, mistreated and diminished yet he kept on working with the people and seeking to humbly resolve the issues.

When bitterness, guilt and offence rise up we can often withdraw from the flock. We then get the proverbial "bee in the bonnet" and move away from the source of irritation and effectively cut ourselves off from fellowship, from the body and unwittingly from Christ the head. We must ask why are so many believers alone? Why do they no longer stay with the mob? When we need to be isolated due to medical reasons that is a normal and a healthy thing to do. I am writing this at the time of the Covid-19 Pandemic and recognise that this is a huge issue and even a divisive one for many. We would trust though for those at home isolating that attempts are made by the local church to continue to link with those in such a situation. The current pandemic has given churches many opportunities to do so. To deliberately withdraw in order to watch or listen to a particular teacher who is the only one who apparently has the truth is truly a very problematic situation and needs to be rectified quickly. We can place the screen preacher whom we have no relationship with on a pedestal and end up worshipping them instead of the head of the church. The church must always have a local body expression where people are gathered by the King to learn to get on together. If there is no local church then maybe it is time to plant one in that area!

Too often the reason given for withdrawal is doctrinal and can sound like someone is taking a strong stand for truth in a sea of liberalism. While this is remotely possible this can too easily just be an excuse for being offended and choosing to "nurse the wound" instead of "lancing the boil" as the Bible tells us to. Offence is one of the most commonly used tools in Satan's weaponry. It produces a flow of toxic bitterness that eats away at the stomach lining of our faith. Only the spiritual weapon of forgiveness flowing from a humble heart can overcome it. Only true repentance allowing *"times of refreshing in the presence of the Lord"*[3] can wash away the river of bitterness that we have allowed to build up within our hearts. Forgiveness is also only possible when we gain a fresh understanding of the horror of our own sin that is no longer held to our account because of the sacrifice of Christ. We deserve the fires of hell so focussing on things that we feel we don't deserve has no biblical gospel foundation.

When wounding does happen we have a biblical path to follow. The first step is forgiveness followed by speaking the truth in love. If there is actual sin involved the matter may need to be carried further. Now having said that it is not always so quick, linear or straightforward. I have discovered that many other scenarios can surface which add to the complexity. At odd (and I mean horribly odd!) times the situation may be one of a terrible blindness on the part of the person you are dealing with. There may be a total absence of the biblical call to "submit to one another." Some people find their way onto a team who are very broken and unable to work in with others. Some are on the team who have chosen a sinful path that will only get more corrupted as they go along. When there is a serious situation of prideful arrogance or someone wanting a following to form their own group of "mini disciples" we have a problem and just sitting down talking it through may not cut it. There

---

[3] Acts 3:19-20
Therefore repent and return, so that your sins may be wiped away, in order that times of refreshing may come from the presence of the Lord. BSB

may even be a mocker on the team and the Word tells us not to engage with such a person as they have such a defiant heart they will only hate you as a result.[4] Spiritual issues like this require prayer and wisdom and making sure we have our spiritual armour on as the battle may just be starting to heat up.

Change from the Old Testament to the New Testament

So often we read of the Holy Spirit coming upon individuals such as Gideon, Moses or David and we then read about their exploits. They were powerful individuals who are great examples to us in many ways. In the New Testament though the Spirit is available for all followers of Christ. It is not just for a select few "big names." We can all become mighty warriors together and with one voice as a mighty army shout "arise!" We can all be filled with the Spirit daily by faith declaring that his mercies are new every morning. The context in the NT is strongly corporate as we individually walk with Christ. Jesus didn't do ministry alone, he trained up 12 "fickle and weak" disciples and many others with whom he maintained a strong connection. The tension between individual discipleship and "body development" must never be lost. We stifle the life of the body when we fail to grow in our walk with Christ and we restrict our personal growth when we fail to become part of an active and maturing local body of believers. We all need each other for many different reasons. Lone Ranger Christianity is not generally the will of God. There will be occasions when we may find ourselves alone and not able to have fellowship but even in those situations the head of the body can provide for us in surprising ways as he loves his children building each other up. Work in with a local church, work in with your ministry team, work in with your leadership team. This may require some tough conversations yet if you are teachable and humble and remain in the

---

[4] Proverbs 9:8 Do not rebuke a mocker, or he will hate you; rebuke a wise man, and he will love you.

love of Christ then real spiritual progress can be made. Remain connected to the body of Christ in every sense that it is possible to do so. As we become body people we discover the wonder of life in the Trinity. This holy corporate life we are called to enter into is incredibly ours and one in which we are destined to experience.

The Church is a gathering of many people across the world and over time who are called to be the local expression of the body of Christ in a given area. This body of Christ must value each other and encourage one another in order to mature into the fullness of Christ.

2

The Inner Core Triplet

The Church has a strong core
FAITH, LOVE AND HOPE
WORK, LABOUR, ENDURANCE

---

1 Thessalonians 1:3

We remember before our God and Father your work produced by faith, your labour prompted by love, and your endurance inspired by hope in our Lord Jesus Christ.

If you are in any way keeping up with the latest trends in the fitness world then you would know that our core is extremely important. The idea is if we get our core muscle groups working properly and don't neglect our "abs" then the rest of what we do with our fitness regime will flow so much better with less effort and more strength. This is the case in the church as well. Our passage brings out what the whole of the Bible teaches about the core triplet of faith, love and hope. If the core is not strong we will just focus on other "spiritual muscle groups" and end up having growth and maturity issues and even some "muscle damage" might occur. Let's examine how to grow our core!

1. Work produced by Faith

Each of the core areas has an associated area of focus. In the "faith" muscle group Paul describes the "…**work** produced by faith." All of us know that as believers we are called to serve our saviour, to work for the King, to labour for our master. Yet there is a great deal of confusion as to what this work should look like and how we should go about carrying it out. How do you know you are doing the work of God? How do you know that it is not just your own flesh being propelled by religious fervour resulting in some twisted selfish gain? It is way too easy to mistake enthusiasm for genuine Spirit led service or to mistake long hours of commitment with true service in the vineyard with Christ who gives us rest. It is also possible to sadly not serve Christ at all due to getting the wrong angle on the "Grace and Works" salvation truth.

Here in this inner triplet we gain insight into both the nature of the work and also the driving force behind true christian service. The work is firstly said to be produced by faith which means to be energised by faith alone with the accompanying truth of our work being completely impossible without faith at every point. If our christian work is lacking faith at every twist and turn then we are basically wasting our time and even possibly "batting for the other team…" which is a scary concept. We really don't want to be doing the devil's work especially when we thought we were following Christ. Satan is our enemy not our co-worker and as such we need to serve God in the only way he intends for us to do so and that is by faith.

Faith must keep on growing

D.L. Moody once said,

"I used to pray daily for the Lord to give me faith. Then one day I read Romans 10:17, which says 'faith comes from hearing, and hearing by the word of God.' So, I began to read my Bible, and faith has been growing ever since."[5]

Faith comes from being in God's word and obeying what we have been given. It comes from delighting in the finished work of Christ and knowing that we are his workmanship created in Christ Jesus to do good works which he prepared in advance for us to do. Those good works come from truly knowing that we are Gods "works of art" and as such we will succeed in whatever endeavours that we through faith are led into. There is a great old phrase which basically says to not forget in the dark what we have been given in the light. In other words when we are reading the word or listening to bible teaching and receive a powerful truth, we must hold onto that truth like a rock hugging barnacle in the intertidal zone when the blistering attacks of the hellish ocean waves crash over our little world. If you have ever tried to extract a barnacle with your bare hands you will find you are in for quite a struggle. We must use the "adductor muscles" of faith to similarly hang tightly onto Christ.

An important question in this whole area relates to the nature of our growing faith and this is best compared to various types of plants. Is my faith a small weed or herb such as parsley or a huge Gum or Oak tree? The former can die very quickly and is very vulnerable to predator attack. The latter are huge powerful trees that offer protection to many species and can withstand vicious storms.

---

[5] StartingwithGod.com "The nature of faith" Dave Lowe

The incredible reality that we must get ahold of is that it is our choice. Are you a Paltry Parsley Person or an Enormous Energetic Eucalypt? By faith we can choose the latter as our identity is wrapped up in the mighty prevailing Lion of Judah.

Why do we work for God?

It would be absolutely right to say it is our way of responding back to the love shown to us. It is a person who is loved so much irrepressibly loving back with zeal and passion. We love because he first loved us and we love Christ because there is no love like his love. We love also to please the Father as to see him in our mind's eye beaming at us because what we are doing is his perfect will and gives him great pleasure. We work for God because the goal of our life is a heart obedience expressed by a surrender of our heart and soul and mind and strength.

Yet there is another dimension that Jesus often spoke about. The work of God is also our bread, it is our elemental sustenance! We gain our life and strength and vigour from doing the will of God. Listen carefully to Jesus' words in John 4:34;

"My food is to do <u>the will of God</u> and to finish <u>the work</u> he has sent me to do."

In other words our source of energy, nutrition and vitality (enjoyment of life) is the work itself and especially the completion of that work. It is the discovery, the commencement and completion of such a work that is our very life on this temporal terrestrial planet that is groaning for its redemption just like we are.

Without the will of God being discovered, commenced and continuing in our lives we are malnourished and filling our bodies with junk! To both start and finish the work which is the will of God is truly our food.

It is way too easy to start a work and get discouraged. I know! I have identified at times more with John Mark than I have with Paul or Barnabas and wondered how I could ever be of use again in the kingdom. I had shingles and other issues in our Mission experience in Bolivia back in the 1990's. We came home a little early as we found that the pressures of mission work with all its demands can take its toll on marriage and family. I discovered though the Amazing Grace of Christ and of his love that surpasses knowledge and in doing so have been led to continue, to be stronger and to worship again. I have been there quite a few times also as a pastor and have had to learn this lesson time and again the hard way. Christ though is infinitely patient and gives wisdom without finding fault as James tells us in the early part of his letter.[6]

Have a good look at Isaiah 40:31 as it sums up how to keep on going in the work and not give up. The work at times will appear like nothing is happening yet this promise in Isaiah reminds us that the very waiting will produce a profound change in what we are capable of and give us a powerful endurance beyond measure. In other words the work as such will have many dimensions of waiting inherent within it. Just remember though that it is waiting on the Lord himself that makes all the difference… not just waiting per se.

"Those who wait on (hope in) the Lord will renew their strength. They will rise up (soar) on wings like Eagles, run and not be weary, walk and not be faint."
Isaiah 40:31

What is work for God?

- Not what others insist we should do….necessarily
- Hearing the voice of the Shepherd…this is crucial…and yes, he does use other members of the body to speak to us!

---

[6] James 1:5
Now if any of you lacks wisdom, he should ask God, who gives generously to all without finding fault, and it will be given to him.

- Allowing him to lead us to the area of work…his specific will for us that he has set aside for us…for which we are suited.
- Accepting our gifts… Know if we are a toe, an ear or a kidney! All of us are valuable…necessary in fact… though not always appreciated… hands and kidneys may not get on so well… not much in common to talk about… yet both play indispensable roles.
- Yet also… serving without demanding to be noticed, respected and appreciated! Tougher than you might think…yet possible.
- In other words with only God needing to see… not doing it to be seen by others…which was the issue with the Pharisees and we all have hearts of Pharisees until we are delivered from them.

There are heaps of activities we can get engaged in to be part of the faith community. Do we truly ask God what he wants us to do in a very specific sense? Are we then focussed in order to carry it out? I don't mean general good works as good as they are, but specific and unique tasks that truly extend the kingdom as they are done in faith.

I am reminded of some of the cutting edge ministries that seek to rescue young girls from sexual exploitation throughout the world. One of the many ministries like this springing up is called "Destiny Rescue." Tony Kirwan who began this movement 21 years ago expresses the daily power he receives from above to do such a dangerous "work for Christ." The rescuers have a number of methods of freeing young girls from sexual slavery in Jesus name and set them up for a new life where they can heal, learn to trust again and become followers of Jesus Christ. These are his words;

"When we have abundance, we will rescue. When we lack resources, we will rescue. When we are tired, we will rescue. When everyone else has given up, we will rescue. We have no plan B. We will always work to rescue and help kids stay free."[7]

---

[7] Tony Kirwan. destinyrescue.org.au

We have to be able to complete the following "My calling each day by the captain of the heavenly army is to….?"

It might include any of the following;

- To be an encourager of others who have lost their way
- To use my gift of faith to lift others to a higher level
- To teach the truths of Scripture that brings freedom
- To give generously to extend the kingdom
- To work with broken young people and lift them up
- To meet physical needs…like Dorcas in the book of Acts
- To bring mental health support to the fragile and broken
- To visit and encourage prisoners in our jails
- To add something to this list that is new and fresh…!

It is important to know that there is a real collection **of random religious duties** we can perform. There are multiple ways we could prove to ourselves and others that we have done or continue to do the Lord's work. As Paul reminds us though its is ultimately only the work of faith that counts as everything else is futile no matter how well intentioned it may be.

2. Labour of Love

"Your labour prompted by love…"

The Greek word used here for labour is kopos (κόπος). According to Strong's concordance [8] it is often associated with a toil that wearies, an intense activity that robs us of energy as well as a deep emotional stress and even unbearable grief. It is associated with overwhelming distress and great burdens. Quite likely we could then say the "Thessalonian Triplet Team" remember how weary their sacrificial love made them

---

[8] 2873

yet they persisted out of the desire to show a true love because that is what Christ is like. Italian cooks say the secret of good cooking is that it is made with love! Make sure you drag the last word out….! Con Amore….Love for the people and even in doing the task itself transforms the food and every other type of labour. Labour has the idea of real strenuous work.

To labour in one area requires not labouring elsewhere.

I had to put a few IKEA "flatpacks" together lately because I love my wife! I was not happy she had bought a flatpack (again) yet the Lord told me that it would be an act of love to do this for her. For me that required intense concentration and endurance though maybe not for you. It required of me to focus exclusively on the task and do no other thing during that time, that I keep going on that one task despite the tedium and the constant nature of the task. To accomplish this "act of love" I had to give up working on any other thing or even to rest. I needed to stay focussed until the "job of love" was done!

Love frequently involves a sacrifice of time and money and resources and energy. Hard work in the kingdom of God is inspired by love. This is only possible when **we walk in the Love of Christ daily.** Our lack of love growing up is healed by opening up our hearts to the love of Christ. This is the heart of Christianity, the gospel, the life of joy. Now what gets in the way of such a way of being? I would have to say many things but especially the following common yet debilitating "devilish" syndrome;

Deficit victim mentality

We cannot allow a "Deficit victim mentality" to control our lives. This is where our most common refrain is;

"I am missing out on or have missed out on such and such and therefore that's why I am like I am and I cannot do a thing about it."

This eventually develops into a "blame" mindset as the reality is we all have "missed out" on different things. Firstly we do need to be honest about the pain of what we wished we had received or experienced yet did not. The honest acknowledgement of this gaping lack is the route to healing. We cannot and must not get stuck in this first step though as that is allowing a wound to fester and many "bitter infections" can result and spread to others. In truth our biggest lack is Christ himself and no person, no experience, no family, no opportunity, and not even some amazing privilege can replace Jesus Christ. He is the one whom we are made to have our life in and without him we are empty. The hollowness and weakness we feel within is not so much due to our lack of input from those around us or some experience but due to not knowing the flow of the Spirit in our lives daily as we abide in Christ by faith. To spend our lives seeking to find ourselves because we sensed we were lost will result in greater loss. Jesus often stressed this truth;

For whoever wants to save his life will lose it, but whoever loses his life for My sake will find it. Matthew 16:25

Jesus is the Good Shepherd who is out searching for us so we must cry out his name. In doing so you will find all you have been looking for. It is not yourself you are looking for it is Christ. Our need is not what our emotions or even deceiving spirits strongly insist we must have. Our need is spiritual and He is the **Holy** Spirit, not lying **unclean** spirits. As we allow the warmth and radiance and unconditional nature of his sacrificial agape love into our hearts we can labour with love. We can toil and sacrifice and give and expend our energy and be emotionally taxed because our love cup is being constantly filled up with Christ. He longs to fill us up with clear, pure water from above that refreshes us like nothing else can. [9]

---

[9] "…That times of refreshing may come from the presence of the Lord." Acts 3:20

3. The endurance of Hope

The Greek word for endurance is hupomone.[10] This term (ὑπομονή) is described below in Thayer's Lexicon[11];

> *In the N. T. the characteristic of a man who is **unswerved from his deliberate purpose** and his loyalty to faith and piety by even the greatest trials and sufferings. A patient, **steadfast waiting** for the return of Christ from heaven.*

True hope enables us to keep going. There is no element of doubt in Christian hope. It is actually a knowing, not a maybe. The person who endures with hope keeps eternity in mind and Jesus' return as our hope. Knowing the brevity of this life and the wonder of eternity is crucial. Francis Chan does a great illustration of eternity.

He describes a very long white rope with a little red bit at the end. This earthly life he says is like the red bit which he then compares to an amazing eternity represented by the very long white rope effectively without end. He encourages us to consider where we should be putting our emphasis. This of course means living an unnatural life of faith and not living by the natural ever present sense of sight.

Hope knows how the story is going to end and that the end is really just the beginning. Hope keeps an eye on the beautiful future that lies before us despite the crushing ugliness of a world that is on fire, quite literally in many places even as I type. As wars and conflicts abound, as persecution increases around the world, as floods and famine and earthquakes and tsunamis increase we are called to do the following;

Be Still and know that I am God
Psalm 46:10

---

[10] #5281 in Strong's concordance
[11] THAYER'S GREEK LEXICON, Electronic Database. Copyright © 2002, 2003, 2006, 2011 by Biblesoft, Inc.

God is moving forward with his perfect programme while Satan and sin and death swirl around his heels. Jesus was bitten on the heel at the cross by Satan but the head of the serpent was also crushed at the cross. This is the promise of victory, of life eternal, of perfection and of righteousness. Back in the 1980's I loved listening to Scott Wesley Brown on a scratchy LP sing the following song;

Then he comes

> *Standing on the edge of human history*
> *Robed in white too bright for mortal eyes*
> *Waiting to reveal the ageless mystery*
> *Ready to roll back the eastern skies*
>
> *Myriads of angels poised around Him*
> *As His lightning steed prepares to ride the wind*
> *And the chains of sin that never could confound Him*
> *Are trampled as the victory march begins*
>
> *Then He comes! He returns!*
> *With a trumpet blast*
> *He comes at last*
> *To take His chosen home*
> *Then He comes! He returns!*
> *It's the end of time*
> *And all war and crime is done*
> *When He comes!*
>
> *All creation waits in silent wonder*
> *For the moment all will be made new*
> *And with the growing sound of righteous thunder*
> *The King of Kings comes swiftly into view*

This song is all about the hope of Jesus return. It is a powerful force given to us by the Lord himself to survive this broken world. Have a look at Romans 8 and take note of the phrase "Who hopes for what he already has?"

24 For in this hope we were saved. But hope that is seen is no hope at all. Who hopes for what they already have? 25 But if we hope for what we do not yet have, we wait for it patiently.

This patient waiting is only possible as we participate and cooperate with the Holy Spirit's work of making us more and more holy, set apart and living in Christ each day. This is what John in 1 John 3 meant when he said that he who has this hope in him purifies himself as he is pure;

2 Dear friends, now we are children of God, and what we will be has not yet been made known. But we know that when Christ appears, we shall be like him, for we shall see him as he is. 3 All who have this hope in him purify themselves, just as he is pure.

Looking to Christ and his return changes everything. We can patiently hope as the return of Christ is getting closer all the time.

The Church is called to develop a strong core. As we work and serve and labour through the spiritual power of faith, hope and love we overcome all the evil one might throw at us.

3
The Power Triplet

The Church is powerful
POWER, SPIRIT, CONVICTION

---

1 Thessalonians 1:5

"…for our gospel did not come to you in word only, but also in power and in the Holy Spirit and with complete conviction…"

This is about the gospel

- The solution to the "world on fire" …"
- The way out of the "deluge of bad news…"
- The antidote to the terror being unleashed around the world by dictators, authoritarian regimes and perplexed and frightened leaders….
- The gospel is the person of Jesus Christ.
- It is the life of the inner person … a life of joy …irrespective of the horror around us.

- The re-orientation back toward the giver of life ... the one who is the Alpha and the Omega... the holder of the keys of life....
- The recognition that a price had to be paid for rebellion and treason in the highest court in the land
- The acknowledgement that only the Son of God in his perfection and obedience could set us free from sin, guilt and shame...
- The power of the blood of Christ and the need for the cross

Framed by 2 "knowings"

It is important to see the slices of bread in which the meat of this truth lies. Verses 4 and 5b are not disconnected, they are in fact highly relevant. Both these two contextual verses indicate two different aspects of this power triplet, of the way the gospel works.

Examine the "sandwich" below where verses 4 - 5b are wrapped around the "filling" of verse 5a.

> 4 For **we know,** brothers and sisters loved by God, that he has chosen you,

5a because our gospel came to you not simply with words but also with power, with the Holy Spirit and deep conviction.

> 5b **You know** how we lived among you for your sake.

First knowing ....top slice of bread

1. We are Loved and chosen

Knowing "...dearly loved brothers" that God has called you, chosen you, elected you.

God has always loved us, it is not a recent thing. He hasn't slowly come around to loving us. He didn't warm to us after a trial period. He didn't start to see things in us he hadn't noticed before.

He loves us now, he always has and he always will for God is love. He loves without any restriction, without limit, without stinginess.

He doesn't love just when we start to do some good stuff as his love is truly unconditional.

Faith receives this love morning by morning and faith loves back and holds onto such a loving one with all our "…mind and heart and soul and strength."

Mark 12:29-31 – "Jesus answered, 'The foremost is, 'Hear, O Israel! The Lord our God is one Lord; and you shall love the Lord your God with all your heart, and with all your soul, and with all your mind, and with all your strength.' The second is this, 'You shall love your neighbour as yourself.' There is no other commandment greater than these.'"

Knowing "dearly loved brothers" that God has called you, that he has chosen you, means in older biblical language that **he has elected you. This whole area of "election" has been a battlefield inside and outside the church for generations.** It is a vivid and shocking reality that the most precious truths are the most attacked and vilified. The most important truths are the most avoided and replaced with shallow alternatives which do not cause any resistance or turbulence among the masses. The waters are so muddied in this area yet clarity is possible so we can drink "great draughts" of sweet pure waters flowing from the mountain streams of heaven that this truth reveals. God has chosen us deliberately and thoughtfully and with great care. He has chosen us because he loves us and wants to pour out his love upon us. He has chosen us to have us respond back to him in love and live daily in his love.

Most of us have memories of not being picked for a sporting team;

- Waiting for our name to be called
- Watching others go forward to join Helen's team or Bazza's side…
- Then came that awful phrase "you can have her… or red shirt."
- Possibly it was worse… "would you like to sit out Melody?" Or "James, would you mind being the scorekeeper?"

Nowadays we might feel deeply for the one not chosen and in this context it is a negative.

Yet it is this very limited scenario that can keep us from embracing the gospel of truth and love. We can be inclined to only focus on poor Robert or Nikisha and in doing so we miss out on so much. Let me explain or at least attempt to do so. The other half of this tension in Scripture also shows that I can choose Christ. I can look at the cross and know in my heart that he died for me and I can say yes to him. It is not all one way or all another way. It is totally both. Yet there is something even bigger than this. It is the wisdom of God. God in his loving wisdom has chosen us. We have felt his Spirit move in our hearts, warming us to his love. Do we reject this love because we are so angry at God for not just picking everyone? Do we demand he does things differently? Do we in our high brow intellectualism insist he got it wrong? Do we say that because we have a Masters or higher in such and such that we know better?

Have a glance or maybe reflect at length on the revelation of who actually makes up of the body of Christ;

26 Brothers, consider the time of your calling: Not many of you were wise by human standards; not many were powerful; not many were of noble birth. 27But God chose the foolish things of the world to shame the wise; God chose the weak things of the world to shame the strong. 28He chose the lowly and despised things of the world, and the things

that are not, to nullify the things that are, 29so that no one may boast in His presence.[12]

Are we willing to not be loved for eternity by God because of our tiny little "puffed up" perspective on this matter? Remember that the one who thinks he knows does not know as he ought to know![13] It is a thing of great beauty that the Creator King has chosen us to live with him forever, to walk in love and to enjoy his presence.

We must walk by faith and trust him in his infinite wisdom. We must steadfastly believe that he will always do what is right, never do wrong and never cause harm as he is perfect in all of his ways. Let us confess our arrogance and cold heartedness though we might think we actually are displaying the opposite. Unfortunately so much resistance to biblical truth is out of an upside down sense of justice and fairness. Let us delight in being the chosen of God and draw as many other sinners into the arms of the Father as he has decreed. Only a person who acknowledges the divine perfect wisdom of God will ever delight themselves in such an important truth. How did Paul and the triplet team know that they were loved by God and chosen specifically by name by him? The answer is found in the power triplet! This power triplet is proof positive that we and them are chosen by God as a result of his deep and continuing love for us. Before we examine the power triplet though let's not forget the bottom slice of bread.

The second knowing....bottom slice of bread

This is clearly not referring to the very British "upper crust" and "lower crust" classification of all people in order to have clear delineations in society! The bottom slice of bread is about how the triplet team

---

[12] 1 Corinthians 1:26-29.
[13] 1 Corinthians 8:2. Those who think they know something do not yet know as they ought to know.

of Paul, Silas and Timothy actually lived their lives. This is essentially a major theme of not just this epistle but many of Paul's letters. How we live among those whom we are trying to reach is fundamental to seeing people brought through for the gospel. Lives of hypocrisy and irrelevance will cause the "middle filling…the gospel in this case" to fall out onto the ground as people reach out to take a bite! Remember the epitaph of the life of Samuel;

And Samuel grew, and the LORD was with him, and He let none of Samuel's words fall to the ground.[14]

This was because his godly authentic life matched up to the message he delivered from above. How does all this work?

"…for our gospel did not come to you in word only, but also in power and in the Holy Spirit and with complete conviction…"

Paul calls the gospel "our gospel." Is he allowed to do this? Well… this is the breathed out word of God…so yes!

We don't get the luxury of deciding whether we prefer Mark or James or Peter or Paul as our Scripture writers. They all were chosen to write as the Holy Spirit inspired them yet they were not machines so they maintained their own personalities, experience and grammatical style. God does not over-ride our unique wiring but instead blows by his Spirit through the fenestrations[15] of our earthly curtain. When Paul uses the pronoun **"our"** he means a shared gospel, one in which they all belong to. The use of the collective pronoun encapsulates a life and truth and body of teaching about the son of God that is bigger than any one person or group of people. It also means that both he and his triplet

---

[14] 1 Samuel 3:19
[15] Merriam Webster dictionary;
"an opening in a surface (such as a wall or membrane)." It is from the Latin for window.

team and all the newly planted churches have been overtaken by the tsunami of the love of Christ. They and all lovers of the truth have been swept up into this gospel as a mighty force for good. He is not saying though that other gospels are fine and everyone is entitled to believe whatever they want. In fact he goes to great pains to say that if even an angel preached another gospel let them be accursed! [16]There is only one gospel and there is no other name by which we might be saved.[17]

The Gospel and Words!

"...did not come to you **in word only**"

Does the gospel contain words? Does it consist of words?

The gospel does require words but many want to just leave it as a carefully constructed grouping of such words. The gospel is so much more than just the right words placed in a careful order and said in a certain way. Words historically though have been incredibly important causing great healing yet also terrible harm. With words whole countries have been swept away into error or truth, fear or freedom or even launched into courage or conflict. The right word at the right time can make all the difference. A wise person carefully selects their words and will adopt a tone that suits the occasion.

Listen to this proverb by wise Solomon;

A word fitly spoken is like apples of gold in settings of silver.[18]

---

[16] Galatians 1:8 But even if we or an angel from heaven should preach a gospel other than the one we preached to you, let them be under God's curse! 9 As we have already said, so now I say again: If anybody is preaching to you a gospel other than what you accepted, let them be under God's curse!

[17] Acts 4:12 Salvation exists in no one else, for there is no other name under heaven given to men by which we must be saved."

[18] Proverbs 25:11. BSB

In another situation a wise person might choose to not utter a single word or choose a few select words than to gush over someone with verbiage.[19] Knowing how to articulate the gospel using the right words is also important as there are many false gospels out there each with different definitions of sin and guilt and salvation.

A common example might be that sin by some is defined as using a plastic bag when you do the shopping. Personally I have basically made the shift to using Hessian bags instead of plastic bags and feel I am doing my bit! [20]This redefining of evil away from a true definition of what God calls sin towards our own personal definitions of wrong happens in many areas. I do not feel that it is "sin" per se to not use a Hessian bag. It is a personal choice to value the environment. Sin arises out of the sinful nature and is a rejection of holiness and a stubborn dependence on self effort. Sin is contrary to the nature of God and holds us captive to its tormenting ways until we are delivered by the sin bearer, our saviour Jesus Christ. We must remember and keep close to our hearts that THE WORD is Jesus Christ himself, not just a group of words on paper or memorised or even treasured. He is THE WORD because through him the Father communicates the totality of himself. All we need to know about God is found in the communique that is Emmanuel meaning "God with us." God didn't just send a book to save us with lots of great thoughts he actually sent his very own son. All the same the Scriptures are breathed out from God, they are for our edification, our discipline and our encouragement. They are special revelation through the prophets and the apostles and other holy writers. They have the privileged task of revealing his Son. There is an old hymn by Mary Lathbury which includes the line "beyond the sacred page I seek thee

---

[19] not verbage as is commonly said...the latter is not actually a real word and sounds more like a herb!

[20] Since the writing of this chapter WA has introduced a ban on plastics bags in supermarkets. Before the ban it was a conscience decision...or maybe a convenience decision... more accurately!

Lord." The song of great devotion is too beautiful to not give you a few more verses;

> Break Thou the bread of life, dear Lord, to me,
> As Thou didst break the loaves beside the sea;
> **Beyond the sacred page I seek Thee, Lord;**
> **My spirit pants for Thee, O living Word!**
>
> Bless Thou the truth, dear Lord, to me, to me,
> As Thou didst bless the bread by Galilee;
> Then shall all bondage cease, all fetters fall;
> And I shall find my peace, my all in all.
>
> Thou art the bread of life, O Lord, to me,
> Thy holy Word the truth that saveth me;
> Give me to eat and live with Thee above;
> Teach me to love Thy truth, for Thou art love.
>
> Oh, send Thy Spirit, Lord, now unto me,
> That He may touch my eyes, and make me see:
> Show me the truth concealed within Thy Word,
> And in Thy Book revealed I see the Lord.

It is wonderful to get our gospel words sorted out but only if it draws us nearer and nearer to THE WORD himself. The gospel is about the love of Christ, not the defence of a philosophy or list of commands or even a belief system on its own.

Now let's do the next bit of the verse and prayerfully not just with words! Words alone will not do it in the kingdom of God as we also need the accompanying power of the Spirit. Just as a sword needs someone to pick it up, skilfully use it and deal the death blow so it is with the words of the gospel which deal the life blow in this case!

I remember a testimony given by a new bible college student who said they had enrolled because they didn't know enough about how to respond to people when asked questions about the bible and the gospel message. I remember thinking that's fine as long as they don't think that the knowledge and information itself will do the convincing. It is always the work of the Spirit, not our capacity to be articulate and have all the right arguments that wins people to Christ. Apologetics is important but I think on some occasions it could be to make Christians feel better about themselves rather than to actually look to the Spirit to take the word shared in genuine love.

A surprising Greek Word

Paul uses an interesting word when he says "did not come to you in words only"

The word the Holy Spirit through Paul used for "**come**" is ginomai (γίνομαι) which means "to become" or "to appear" or even "to be born". The idea is to change from one state or condition into another so has the idea of transformation or conversion inherent within it. If the concept of "arriving at a destination" was the main thought then most likely the verb erchomai (ἔρχομαι) would then have been used. So the idea is the words of the Gospel that the missionary triplet shared did not just stay as mere words, as great thoughts and ideas or even as elevated philosophy but they "became" something of great power. True, they were always powerful but as we know from experience words alone do not save us from sin, the powerful work of Christ alone does. We might "deliver" the message but a "convicting and transforming" work must go on in order for the heart to be softened, the mind to be opened and for the rebirth to occur. Luke records that as Lydia heard the words of the gospel "…the Lord opened her heart to respond to Paul's message." [21]

---

[21] Acts 16:14

The gospel words don't just travel from our mind through our lips to the ears of the hearer as if that's the whole story! They must be <u>transformed</u> into agents of power and conviction. Many people have heard the gospel and it has had no positive effect. Many have shunned the message. Many have rejected Christ.

- So how does the message powerfully become an agent of rebirth?
- How does it become a surgeon's scalpel that does spiritual surgery?
- How does it become food that is nourishing?
- How does it become fresh pure water that gives incredible refreshment?

For the answers to these questions let's now examine the power triplet! They work "in sync" with the Word of God, with the gospel truths. More than that they give the Word of God a transforming miraculous capacity that demonstrates that what is said is true.

"but also in power and in the Holy Spirit and with complete conviction..."[22]

Listen to the prophet Jeremiah;

28 Let the prophet who has a dream recount the dream, but let the one who has my word speak it faithfully. For what has straw to do with grain?" declares the Lord. 29 "Is not my word like fire," declares the Lord, "and like a hammer that breaks a rock in pieces?[23]

We want to see God's own sword, his word, burn like a fire in the hearts of men and women and children. We cannot be content to just see a flickering spark that emits a minuscule display of human generated phosphorescence. As pastors we must not be content with well con-

---

[22] 1 Thessalonians 1:5
[23] Jeremiah 23:28, 29

structed sermons and thoughtful nods accompanied by the occasional burst of laughter or a few tears. Youth pastors must not be satisfied with just becoming amazing communicators using all the tools gleaned from TED talks[24] and stand-up comedians that keep our audience spellbound. We want to see the Word of God, the gospel, shared with the force of a hammer and exhibiting the intensity of a raging bushfire. We will then see hardened stony hearts and stubborn resistance reduced to rubble allowing a repentance and sorrow for sin and a warmth toward God flood in with heavenly healing. This is what happened when Peter and Paul lived out the gospel and it can happen with every Christian who understands that words must be delivered with the power of a genuine Spirit filled life. As we have been emphasising all along this is most effective when done in prayerful unity with other believers.

1. WITH POWER

Acts 16

Cast your mind to the jailer in Philippi who saw the power of God fall in a fortified prison. After much suffering and mistreatment endured by the Apostles and after a choice to allow joy to enter into their apparent tragedy something amazing happened. Despite a great difficulty possibly accompanied with a natural temptation to believe God had abandoned them they instead rejoiced and sung through the pain. It was right at that point that a miracle occurred! Here we see the power of God enter into a situation in a way that no-one expected. Paul and Silas did not demand that God rescue them from their plight or claim that the doors fling open by the power of impressive visualisation techniques. This incredible event was a miracle that was out of the ordi-

---

[24] Technology, Entertainment and Design are great areas to learn in yet Preaching is entirely different. One is earth bound the other needs to flow from heaven. True preaching requires marinating in Scripture and walking in the Spirit.

nary and completely revealed the mysterious and explosive power of the transcendent God. It was the faith filled lives of the believers that ultimately precipitated the powerful miracle from above. The power is clearly not from the believers yet it is enabled and released by the faith of the believers. The call is to trust when things are messy and tough and nasty and not to demand that they (or we) be immediately released from the nasty situation. It is so much better to calmly look around for a miracle of God's sovereign appointment and continue to wait on God.

Remember the second lower crust of the sandwich?

4 For we know, brothers and sisters loved by God, that he has chosen you, 5a because our gospel came to you not simply with words but also with power, with the Holy Spirit and deep conviction. 5b**You know how we lived among you for your sake.**

It is the faith filled authentic life of the believer who has responded to the overpowering love of God that enables and releases the power of God into a situation. Don't believe it…? Have another read of the New Testament and you will begin to see this link.

2. WITH THE HOLY SPIRIT

What is being said here? Only the most important thing a witness, a preacher and every believer must know with conviction! If we ever think that just by knowing the ideas, principles and thoughts of the Bible more and more clearly that we will win people for Christ… then heaven help us! If you ever thought that by having more ministries and outreach events that the church would just automatically somehow fill up then we have missed the point of how people come to Christ and how they grow and become disciple makers themselves. We have also put our focus on numbers and if that is our primary focus we are already in trouble even and maybe especially if our church does grow numerically!

People come to Christ by the work of the Holy Spirit who uses the Word of God that is being lived out, contextualised and spoken in a local dialect in a natural way by his people. If Acts 1:8 means anything it means that we are not to ever think that just by learning the gospel truths and becoming more proficient at declaring truth that we will ever break through the defences of the kingdom of darkness and see the kingdom of light shine forth.

8 **But you will receive power when the Holy Spirit comes on you**; and you will be my witnesses in Jerusalem, and in all Judea and Samaria, and to the ends of the earth.

Walking by faith is walking in the power of the Spirit which is walking by faith! It is the difference between just pushing a car and in comparison turning on the motor that has a tank filled with fuel with a fully charged battery.

Car Manual devotional

Depending on the words alone, the Word of God alone, is like telling everyone about the nice new car that you've just purchased. We then push it to work and push it back while stopping every so often to have a 'devotional' of the car manual and then we begin to push again! We know how powerful this new car is with its V8 motor but we insist on pushing it because we don't know what else to do. We believe in its power but can't quite work out why it isn't roaring along at great speed and flying up the hills! A devotional time with the King of Kings that leaves us just as weary and lost and lacking in direction afterwards is a misnomer. It is not being devoted to Christ at all. It is just reading holy words and looking for inspiration and perhaps enjoying some religious feelings. We then return back to what we were doing as if there had been no connection at all to the greatest source of love and power and refreshment available in the universe. Perhaps its time to get a vision like Ezekiel had on the Kebar river. When the igniting spark of the Spirit is present … wow! We have movement and the Christian life is not so exhausting.

Sometimes we are like the following person who said;

"I'm just waiting for heaven…or the rapture[25].… I'm exhausted…it couldn't come quick enough as far as I'm concerned!"

We must know in our very beings that this is only Holy Spirit work. It is his specialty, it is his priority, it is his desire. We must be totally dependent on him. That means becoming people who live in prayer at all times. We are called to pray in the morning, throughout the day and all through the night being dependent on the Spirit for all things.

It is our natural human dependence on our own capacities that kills the work of the gospel. It also causes us to become either hypocritical, cynical or just plain sad. We must cry out with desperation for the salvation of those around us and also use words and live out our lives as we die to self.

The twin errors

There seems to be two "equal and opposite" errors that we can fall into as we seek to share the gospel of Christ. The first of these is not being able to shake the feeling that we are ever quite knowledgeable enough or articulate enough to bring someone to Christ therefore holding back out of inadequacy and fear. The other possibly even more debilitating error has a self congratulatory aspect to it. We might feel that we have shared so much truth in so many ways to our unbelieving friends and co-workers and family that having done "…a pretty good job even if we do say so ourselves…which we probably do" we feel that there is

---

[25] Much more to be said about the rapture later in Paul's letter. There is a lot of negative talk on this topic which I believe is based on some misunderstandings that need to be clarified.

nothing more we can do now so it is finally time to let God in on the picture.

Both of these are faulty as they are not Spirit centred but human centred! The first refuses to step out and live a faith filled life. The second steps out with a bag full of training, enthusiasm and skills yet forgets that it is not by human might in any form that changes the hearts and minds of rebel human beings it is only the Spirit of God!

It is only a complete dependence on the Spirit to work, demanding that we pray with faith that we will see people being saved. It is not just our own work that we are talking about here. As has been often said we are called into writing Acts 29. This means the continuing ACTS of the resurrected Christ are done through the ACTS of the Holy Spirit displayed by the ACTS of Spirit filled, Christ exalting believers working in unity as a church that ACTS right up until the return of Christ.

3. WITH GREAT CONVICTION

The Greek word plérophoria (πληροφορία) means with full assurance, conviction and confidence. It implies that there is no doubt, there is a grasping with both hands, there is a heart flung wide open, there is no reticence or uncertainty.

Here are the first 2 verses of Blessed Assurance[26] which is a song of great emotion and conviction.

> Blessed assurance, Jesus is mine
> Oh, what a foretaste of glory divine
> Heir of salvation, purchase of God
> Born of His Spirit, washed in His blood

---

[26] The Lyrics were written by Fanny Crosby and composed by her friend Phoebe Knapp in 1873.

> Perfect submission, all is at rest
> I in my Saviour, am happy and blessed
> Watching and waiting, looking above
> Filled with His goodness, lost in His love.

This is when you know that things are real, when you know finally you have discovered the truth that you've been searching for all your life. The journey has ended yet has just begun! The Thessalonians saw it in the eyes and the faces and the lives of these three travelling missionaries. These three foreigners who were not welcomed by the majority. These three preachers who gave a message that was both the very message all Jews had learnt their whole lives and another message that they had never heard before. This message that the one longed for and promised had truly come yet had been brutally killed. This horrifying message had a powerful twist though; the Messiah had resurrected and it was now clear that this had been the divine plan all along. Astonishingly all of this was and still is true and it makes all the difference to my life and to yours as now his very own life can be ours. This astonishing mystery was now revealed and made very plain in power.

They were convinced and convicted in a very short period of time. They had no doubt, they were assured! They were not encountering just another idea, another philosophy or another religion. They had finally found the truth and the truth was a person. Jesus is the Way, the Truth and the Life! They now knew it and absolutely nothing held them back. Let's find out more of what their faith did to this whole region in the next few chapters.

The church knows that along with the words of the gospel there is the need for the accompanying power by the Holy Spirit which brings deep conviction. The church of the living God recognises its power comes from the Spirit of God convicting hearts and minds through the word in our midst.

4

The Worship Triplet

The Church worships the living and True God
TURN, SERVE, WAIT

---

1 Thess 1: 9-10

5c... You know how we lived among you for your sake. **6** You became imitators of us and of the Lord, for you welcomed the message in the midst of severe suffering with the joy given by the Holy Spirit. **7** And so you became a model to all the believers in Macedonia and Achaia. **8** The Lord's message rang out from you not only in Macedonia and Achaia—your faith in God has become known everywhere. Therefore we do not need to say anything about it,

9 for they themselves report what kind of reception you gave us. They tell how you turned to God from idols to serve the living and true God, 10 and to wait for his Son from heaven, whom he raised from the dead—Jesus, who rescues us from the coming wrath.

There is an important "contextual triplet" which must not be missed in order to understand the worship triplet. We find it immediately before our passage in verses 5c-8. Paul speaks of the gospel being lived out in its fullness like a drama or play that shows in detail the way this new life really works. It is an experienced "tradie" being watched by a keen apprentice or a "top surgeon" being followed around by a group of interns eager to observe every small detail to become even more proficient. The true discipleship process is revealed here in just a few verses. The new life is lived out and then imitated with the "check" of the Holy Spirit. The new believers lives became a model to all those in the region. A region is then "evangelised" for Christ. Here is the contextual triplet in short;

> **Living**…not just words…being conduits of power from above displaying what they were teaching…inviting others into the joy
> **Imitating**…humility is required to do this… despite suffering… strengthened with joy…looking to the Lord at all times
> **Modelling**…as they were taught so they modelled…and others saw the new life and were reached with the gospel…..the apprenticeship model!

Result… The ringing out of the gospel… like a loud bell… everywhere!

Question: What is the sign is that the Spirit is at work in an area?

Answer: Hearing people talking about how distinct and different we all are!

This means not trying to be clones of the world to reach the world. It also means not trying to be clones of other churches that have abandoned or at least neglected the Word of God for worldly and even more sensational means of growth. Let's be disciples who stand out and draw people in and not try to be just another "same old" flickering light or "new shiny glow" to try and fit in and end up losing our saltiness. There is a way to be a distinctive church but it requires a commitment to the Word of God and a willingness to be different in the way Christ wants. We must not be a clanging cymbal but instead be a "bell that rings out a message" as the living and the imitating was out of love. Examine carefully the nature of what was said about these firebrand Thessalonians;

> Turn, Serve and Wait….
> They were known as worshippers.
> This is what made them distinct.

What do churches today sometimes want to be known as?

> Contemporary…not having archaic ideas
> Relevant…speaking the language of the world
> Approachable…in other words "not weird"
> Concert holders…a lively performance
> Acceptable….Just like the world… only nicer
> Community…where we are free to be ourselves

Many of these things are fine on the surface but they must be put under careful biblical scrutiny. If they are intentionally made to be the core values of a church without wise discernment then true biblical worship takes a back seat and eventually is not even welcome in the church at all.

At the heart of this is a true understanding of worship.
Worship is Inherent in all those made in the image of God.
It is divinely planted deeply within our inner being. The word of God teaches us that we become like whom we worship.[27] We are created to give ourselves totally to something outside of ourselves hence

---

[27] Psalm 115:8 Those who make them will be like them, and so will all who trust in them.

the constant need to build up an idol of any kind in our lives. We cannot decide with our own reasoning though what is best for us as it is not random or self determined. Remember Augustine who said we all have a God shaped vacuum within us that cannot be filled with anything besides our creator. Other religions have arisen out of this need to worship as it is implanted from above. Fear though is often at the heart of their worship as Satan thrives and builds his kingdom on intimidation and terror. Worship can be of our bodies or our families or even the protective cocoon of our privileged lifestyle.

We worship what we hold up the highest and hang onto the tightest.

So to truly worship three things must occur. This worship triplet sums up true holy worship. Anything that lacks these three things is not godly worship no matter what we might call it.

1. Turn from Idols

An idol is anything that replaces a deep giving of ourselves to Christ.

Even worshipping an apostle, a saint or an angel is idolatry as it is giving worship to others besides the King of Kings. The ten commandments instruct us to not make for ourselves a graven image which is an idol and bow down to it.[28]

What then is an idol in general terms?

- Whatever gets us up in the morning
- Whatever lights our fire
- Whatever we hate giving up
- Whatever we feel is the core of who we are
- Whatever fills us with fear if we do not submit to it

---

[28] You shall not make for yourself an idol in the form of anything in the heavens above, on the earth below, or in the waters beneath.5You shall not bow down to them or worship them; Exodus 20:4-5

- To lose it is to lose ourselves…this is an idol.
- Many of those things need at least a serious priority re-adjustment as our "first love" has been lost and given to another.

How can I put what has become an idol at the feet of Jesus?

You can't tell me sport or music are not some of the biggest idols in Australian society, along with of course the environment. God is into music and sport and ecology yet it is all about what our greatest passion is. Romans 1 is pretty strong about worshipping the creator and not the created;

25 They exchanged the truth about God for a lie, and worshipped and served created things rather than the Creator—who is forever praised. Amen.

Job also describes how wicked it is to be enchanted by the heavenly bodies instead of giving glory to the creator;

if I have regarded the sun in its radiance
   or the moon moving in splendour,

27
so that my heart was secretly enticed
   and my hand offered them a kiss of homage,

28
then these also would be sins to be judged,
   for I would have been unfaithful to God on high.[29]

Just watch supposedly "non-religious" footy fans at a match. They are normally very sane and controlled yet will suddenly burst out with a passion that is phenomenal. When 90 000 people explode with joy or

---

[29] Job 31:26-28

sorrow all at once it is a palpable experience which is brimming with life. It not wrong to display such passion…keep doing it ! We have to ask though what is it that gets our primary exuberant celebration by expressing what lies deep within us? Is Christ more thrilling than your favourite singer belting out your favourite song or your footy team getting into the grand final or kicking a goal that gives them the game ? This of course is only possible as the Spirit daily fills us, transforms us and reshapes us.

How is that thrill and joy and celebration expressed in the church?

Yes, it is true, reverence and awe and stillness must be present but if we are turning from idols and we are made for celebration then just how does a church truly move ahead in this area? An extraordinary truth is that there is a version of christianity which produces depressed and even harsh people. Such people rightly know that all other exuberance must not be misplaced as God is the only one who deserves such a display of affection. This of course is half of the truth tension and must not be ignored. Deep down though proponents of such a mentality have no true passion left for Christ due to being emotionally stunted and relationally closed. This results in God's people who are promised great joy becoming the saddest people on earth! We are then to be pitied more than anyone for we are truly joyless! Why would anyone want to turn from their idols and become like us if we are more sour than a cumquat?[30]

When Herod received the worship of a god this is what happened;

Then Herod went from Judea to Caesarea and stayed there. 20 He had been quarreling with the people of Tyre and Sidon; they now joined together and sought an audience with him. After securing the support of Blastus, a trusted personal servant of the king, they asked

---

[30] Cumquat info… a very small tart citrus fruit that can make you screw up your face!

for peace, because they depended on the king's country for their food supply.
21 On the appointed day Herod, wearing his royal robes, sat on his throne and delivered a public address to the people. 22 They shouted, "This is the voice of a god, not of a man." 23 <u>Immediately, because Herod did not give praise to God, an angel of the Lord struck him down, and he was eaten by worms and died.</u>
24 But the word of God continued to spread and flourish.

When we are extremely successful and accept the worship of others we become an idol to them and keep them from the worship of God that only he is due. Sadly this happens in some churches that appear very successful on the surface and may have had a history of true worship at some stage.

There is a need to CULTIVATE AND COMMIT.

There must be a **Cultivation** of passionate exuberance for the King of Kings coupled with a steely **Commitment** toward Christ that is not based on an emotional response. Deep, holy worship and exuberant joyful praise are both needed in a healthy church.

We must not be held back by some theology which is only partly right. Reverence and celebration must be both present in large doses.

2. Serve the living and true God

This facet of service was clearly obvious and distinctive.

It was something worth pointing out and noticed by outsiders who even talked about it among themselves.

It was a change that took them by surprise.

They "paid homage" to a different God!

They weren't serving what or whom they used to serve.

To serve is to be committed to someone outside of ourselves. To serve is to spend time doing what pleases the master. It was and still is very natural to serve ourselves, to serve number one, to just look after our own family.

To serve is to be deliberate and intentional in our activity which is the will of the Father. To serve is to have found out specifically what we are supposed to obey in. True service must be out of faith or it is "still under law". Service as such has also been somewhat lost or at least re-packaged in the contemporary church. **Churches can now be set up as Consumer Churches.** We should define such a church as it is very tempting to become one. In fact it Is touted in some quarters as being the only way to grow and be relevant.

CONSUMER CHURCH DEFINED

A consumer church is based on the premise that people's wants must come first and be the primary factor in how a church is designed and envisioned. People are pictured as walking through the door asking the question "what can I get from this place?" They may even ask "What is here for me and for my family?" Our response may be then to do all we can to facilitate the provision of their consumer needs as if that is the role of the people of God. We stock the shelves with eye catching items and potentially fail to ask God what he wants for his people. We become more like politicians or marketing experts rather than being holy leaders in the church of the resurrected Christ. A church where the WORD and WORSHIP both by the SPIRIT is emphasised asks the question "What does God want?" as well as "How do our people become distinct from the world in order to shine more brightly in the world?"

The "off the shelf" consumer items which are seen by "progressive" churches as indispensable become less important as worship of the Holy One becomes our primary pursuit. The ministries and activities of our church then flow from a heart of holy worship. The core elements are not compromised as the ministries are developed.

A worshipping church then is based on the premise that idols will be forsaken and preached against. A worshipping church is one where people will be led to serve the living God in all sorts of ways that he prescribes and there will be a waiting for his Son from heaven so let's talk about that!

3. Wait for his Son from Heaven

To wait is not a passive experience in the realm of the Spirit.

To wait is to "pass up" other opportunities as what is coming is much better.

Time for an illustration;

Beef Vindaloo fable....(it isn't quite true!)

At a family party Justin wasn't eating the amazing food brought by his aunties. Even uncle Harry's fish curry was being rejected. No-one could work out what was going on as he was generally a ravenous eater. Finally he let everyone know that Uncle Jimmy's new wife was from Mumbai. She makes the most amazing "Bombay Beef" that took him to culinary heaven so as to speak. It was so good it was worth saving himself for in order to have a huge serving of this amazing curry.

To spiritually wait is to practice the much maligned practice of "delayed gratification." To wait is to live in anticipation for what is coming and to not live for this world. To wait is to adjust our lives, our activities and our desires to not be ashamed at his coming.

The new church was confused about those who had already died before Christ returned so Paul cleared that up a bit later in the letter. Yet this very confusion was partly because they were so intently looking forward to the return of Christ. Note here that the church was made up of Jews and Greeks together. Jesus was returning for all his sheep, not just some as the wall of hostility was broken down. To wait is to accept and brush off any scorn. It is accepting you might be mocked for being so irrelevant especially by the trendy "hip hop" Christians. It is highly likely that we are more afraid of the opinions of other churches than we are of what the world might think. We mustn't live out of the fear of "men or women" but instead be prepared to display the life and declare the truth that is in Christ through his word and the Spirit without fear. The waiting for Christ's return will produce scorn at times. Listen to what Peter has to say;

Above all, you must understand that in the last days scoffers will come, scoffing and following their own evil desires. 4 They will say, "Where is this 'coming' he promised? Ever since our ancestors died, everything goes on as it has since the beginning of creation."[31]

A worshipping church will see the Lord's message ring out and be known for its heart of worship. The heart of this worshipping church is based on the premise that Idols will be forsaken and preached against, people will be led to serve the living God in a variety of forms and there will be a waiting for his Son from heaven who is coming with majesty and in judgement.

---

[31] 2 Peter 3: 3

5

The TWO False Motive Triplets

The Church gets its approval from God alone
**ERROR, IMPURITY, TRICKERY &
FLATTERY, GREED COVERING, PRAISE SEEKING**

---

1 Thessalonians 2:1-6

Repenting of unhealthy patterns of ministry

It is seriously possible for the most well intentioned person to have the wrong motives in any christian ministry. We can start off well but "fall off the cart" as we progress for a number of reasons. Just what are these alternative ways to "do ministry" or "work in the church" or "serve God?" How can we be sucked into unhealthy patterns of ministry and even take pride in them? What might these "unity damaging" approaches look like?

Let's read the passage and allow it to unfold.

1 You know, brothers and sisters, that our visit to you was not without results. **2** We had previously suffered and been treated outrageously in Philippi, as you know, but with the help of our God we dared to tell you his gospel in the face of strong opposition. **3** For the appeal we make does not spring from error or impure motives, nor are we trying to trick you. **4** On the contrary, we speak as those approved by God to be entrusted with the gospel. We are not trying to please people but God, who tests our hearts. **5** You know we never used flattery, nor did we put on a mask to cover up greed—God is our witness. **6** We were not looking for praise from people, not from you or anyone else, even though as apostles of Christ we could have asserted our authority.

Firstly let's lay a foundation...

Underneath all of what Paul is about to lay forth is a reminder of their courageous sharing in the face of suffering. This is the bedrock, the deep and enduring foundation of true ministry. It is this willingness to let go of personal security and happiness that brings a healthy harvest. It is this capacity to endure suffering for Christ's sake that sets the direction toward being God pleasers and away from being people pleasers. Being people pleasers loses its appeal when our suffering comes from people and maybe even the very people we are trying to please!

False ungodly motives in the first triplet include;

Error, Impurity and Trickery   2:3

Further false motives in the second triplet include;

Flattery, Wearing of masks and Praise from people 2:5,6

Firstly we need to differentiate between the common usage of the term "people pleasing" and a more biblical sense of this very "bandied around" concept. By biblical I mean "how the bible talks about such and such." In this case we are talking about the idea of "fearing others." There is also a use of the term "biblical" which can just mean "my doctrinal stance" and that is a problematic use of the term. There is a fine line here but I do not believe it to be purely pedantic.

People pleasing (definition 1) is the idea of living with the need for approval of others and being broken whenever that fails to occur which will be most of the time. We frequently let each other down as we are not God. This is not a false definition it is just not the only way the Word of God uses the term.

People pleasing (definition 2….in most of this chapter) is used in the sense of "gaining popular approval" to "gain kudos" in order to "get away with sinful stuff". This could be called the art of manipulation. Paul is then saying that they did not use underhanded means to win them over. Our goal though as believers is in both situations to only live for the approval of the perfect one who has placed us in Christ hence giving us perfect approval. Whenever we seek the approval of others to feel good about ourselves (definition 1) we do not live by faith and instead live by sight: that which we see and feel. This mode of behaviour will undo us so we need to be wary. It is important to realise also that the evil one uses us in our weak moments to hurt each other and so needing the approval of others enables us to play into the hands of the devil. Whenever we use certain means to cause others to look favourably upon us (definition 2) yet our motives are ungodly we also must repent. The call is to then live by faith and turn away from such means to get ahead in ministry and become people who only live for the approval of the Lord. This may be costly but it is the only way that pleases God and is authentic.

First "False motive triplet"

1. Error

"For the appeal we make does not spring from error…"

Error is a departure from the truth, it's just wrong!

Maybe we are one of the 3-D people?

Deluded ...have a wrong sense of perspective and end up in some fantasy land.
Deliberate...we want something so we just plain invent it or twist it or lie.
Discernment issues...due to not walking with Christ and not being in his word has led us to not being able to discern error.

Paul addresses this lack of spiritual discernment elsewhere to Timothy when he described a group of people as "…Always learning but never able to arrive at a knowledge of the truth…."[32]

Just why would we not tell the truth? That is of course a huge question and probably has multiple answers. Here are a few;

A. Pride.

We have discovered a new thing that others don't know about and choose to not investigate any further or allow others to speak into our new discovery….pride.

This type of thinking puffs us up and separates us from the body. When we only ask ourselves the big questions and only listen to our own responses and feelings we can quickly end up believing a lie. Allowing others to challenge our position is crucial for truth to surface.

B. Cult leader mentality

Maybe we deep down love to have a following.

---

[32] 2 Timothy 3:7

The idea of having disciples is too 'heady' and intoxicating' to let go of. If not the cult leader then maybe we are "ready prey" for such a person who recognises your vulnerability and sees the wounds and is able to exploit you through your past hurts. In all of this truth becomes the chief casualty. In the pursuit of a band of followers or enjoying the charisma of a leader who takes us under his or her wing we fall into error.

C. A spirit (spirits) of error

As Satan is the father of lies the idea that certain demons are "deluding spirits" or "spirits of error" cannot be disregarded. We must be able to lay down all thoughts that are not of Christ and his word. We must "cut off" in Jesus name any deceiving spirits that seek to pull us in a wonky direction. This practice of spiritual warfare is crucial if we are to follow Christ into healthy territory for his church.

2. Impurity

"...or impure motives."

This is like when a Father with a teenage daughter asks her new boyfriend what his intentions are! This type of technique that Paul is addressing is probably a desire to achieve unholy and fleshly goals with the appearance of goodness. It is when we are driven by lusts of various kinds and refuse to repent of them, even justifying them or worse taking pride in them.

Maybe we are out to make money, have a sexual encounter or be seen as a powerful influential individual? When someone is not the "full picture" or the "real deal" we can eventually sense that there is something "out of whack." Even though their arguments may be exciting or enticing or "seem to make sense" we begin to back away from their programme and wonder what is actually going on.

If our motives are impure we will end up hurting the people we work among. When the Spirit or other people with the Spirit rebuke us or point out an ugly truth about us we must be grateful and not pretend we have not sinned no matter how embarrassed we might feel. John has a few words to say about that;

6 If we claim to have fellowship with him and yet walk in the darkness, we lie and do not live out the truth. **7** But if we walk in the light, as he is in the light, we have fellowship with one another, and the blood of Jesus, his Son, purifies us from all sin. **8** If we claim to be without sin, we deceive ourselves and the truth is not in us.
1 John 1:6-8

3. Trickery

"...nor are we trying to trick you."

- With a heart set on deception much like a "con artist."
- With a full intent to present a lie with artful manipulation.
- Not done out of faith.
- Not depending on God to provide.
- Yet fully convinced in their own mind that these methods are right and helpful, to be applauded and even using our gifts from God to accomplish such trickery!

Remember the movies featuring the gambler and the hustler as the good guy ripping off the wealthy fat cats and enjoying the thrill of the chase! Such people, and we are all capable of this, have to be capable of great self deception in order to be people of ministry, doing the Lord's work, but not using his means. In the Old Testament there are so many stories which reveal the disastrous consequences of living unholy lives while being seen to do the work of God. Think about Hophni and Phinehas the sons of the godly Eli. They despised the Lord by taking from the sacrifice the rich fatty portions they were not permitted to have. It was also no secret that they were sleeping with the women who served at the entrance to the tent of meeting. It was only for a time that the holy one endured such contempt for his name. The Lord rose up in his perfect timing using their enemy to deal with such trickery. The Philistines took the ark of the covenant in battle and we then read that in the attack they both died on the same day. Phinehas' wife gave birth to a son she called Ichabod meaning "without glory" as the ark had been taken and maybe also because of the "inglorious" and dishonourable life her husband had lived.

Remember Jeremiah's words about our hearts?

The heart is deceitful above all things and beyond cure. Who can understand it? Jeremiah 17:9

Second False motive triplet

4. Flattery

"...You know we never used flattery"

Flattery is such a slippery one as from the surface such activity can appear to be a truly encouraging thing to do. Finally we have someone who sees our value and the good that we do. They must be a good person and clearly God has sent them into our lives!

Flattery is quite literally a steady pouring out of compliments over a person who is undeserving of such praise. They may well know themselves it is not true but they may permit such activity in order to have the other person on side or enjoy a fleeting glow of self belief.

Flattery can be described as being the following;

- The telling of untruths
- A seeking to manipulate

- The classic "buttering up"
- A refusal to live in the real world

Flattery can be considered in our own minds to be a holy and even godly thing to do. We might think that because it is not pulling someone down but lifting them up it must be right.

Just what happens when we exaggerate the goodness of someone or even go beyond and tell them a lie about themselves? Perhaps more importantly just why do we do it?

I believe there are three main reasons why we might activate the flattery switch. In this passage I believe Paul is referring to the third reason more than the others. We might call these reasons **smoke, scratch and shine!**

SMOKE.

Firstly it deflects from our own weaknesses. Our super encouragement becomes a smoke screen to keep the glare off our own failings as we effectively enter into a bargaining arrangement whereby we state very clearly;

"I won't pick on you if you don't pick on me…"

Where there is smoke there is fire so watch out or douse your own unholy fire with a love for Christ that turns away from such means.

SCRATCH.

Secondly it may well be a backhanded way of drawing the other person in so that they respond in kind and gush over us as well. It becomes a mutual admiration club that is based on false praise and therefore is prone to fall apart at any moment.

"If you scratch my back I'll scratch yours. "

It is good to build each other up but let it be done in truth and not used to gain a foothold where we may not be supposed to climb.

SHINE.

Thirdly it is about using a moment of golden glitter to sway the minds of the people. Flattery no longer makes the ministry a level playing field. Ministry evaluation gains the edge of "inflated emotional gloss" which can be convincing to the ignorant, the proud or the weak. Who doesn't want to hear some amazing comment about how we do things or how we speak? The "temporary shiny advantage" is enough to sway many.

"You guys are just amazing, I've never come across any group of people so humble and gifted! We will do really well together especially with my talents in the mix."

The arguments presented by the flattering ministry team or individual are not carefully considered and weighed up as they ought to be. The "praise gushing" group or individual is now given an unhealthy entrance and a hearty welcome based on fleshly means. How subtle all of this can be.

Paul and the team refused to speak anything to the Thessalonians except the message of the gospel in unvarnished truth. They sought to live out their lives in a way that revealed their authenticity and they especially did not throw buckets of false affirmations over a people they were seeking to bring to the foot of the cross and see mature in Christ, who is the way, **the truth** and the life.

5. Mask wearing…to cover greed

In this section the wearing of a mask carries with it the idea of hiding who we really are in order to gain trust. There is a deep knowledge that the person I am needs some serious tweaking as my weaknesses are too great to be real and vulnerable before this group I am seeking to minister among.

Masks are worn to deceive. I'm certainly not talking about face or surgical masks as I type this during the "Covid-19 pandemic." Spiritual masks enable us to operate without getting caught.

Maybe though it is because at times we are unsure of who we even are? We keep on putting on various masks because we are trying to work out our identity. This can be because we refuse to accept the way God has made us which never goes against his word. Living by faith leads to knowing our identity in Christ before we try and become anything or anyone else. It leads to peace in the discovery of who we truly are currently and in time can become.

How can a mask be worn? What does it look like?

I would have to say that if they seem too good to be true they probably are although there is the genuine article of course!

Masks try and represent the opposite of the reality.

As in the case when someone frequently talks about a topic in order to cause people to believe that's what we are really like. Think of Judas who proudly declared "could not this have been sold and the money given to the poor..."[33] the bible says he said this because he was a thief! If the mask is worn to cover up greed the mask will begin to slip over time. We then need to be willing to acknowledge when we see it in others whom we have maybe even begun to admire.

Maybe when someone comes with a mask that we want to see because we've been waiting so long for such a person we refuse to believe the evidence that might be pointing in the opposite direction! Over time we are in love with an idea and happy to believe the mask and just really hope that it's the real deal. Finally when the mask no longer can stay in place we might just be forced to admit the reality of a situation or a person or sadly as some do refuse to believe what we

---

[33] "Why wasn't this perfume sold for three hundred denarii and the money given to the poor?" John 12:5 BSB

actually see before us. The truth is too painful and things would have to be changed and confrontation may well have to occur and that is often just too hard for many.

6. Seeking praise from people

We long for praise from somewhere. Saying we don't care what anyone thinks is trickery in itself. What we really mean when we say such a thing is we have become more selective in who we want approval from or need approval from which of course is a good thing. Deep down we long for praise from people whom we genuinely look up to, admire and respect. That is inbuilt within us.

That person ultimately must be Christ though as everyone else will at some point let us down.

While seeking praise from people is in some ways not a deliberate malicious thing to do it does lead to a life lived by sight, out of the will of God and will lack his power and presence and promise.

We will not have any joy as our happiness becomes dependant on the latest tidbit of encouragement we might have thrown toward us like a chicken bone from the person we have come to need to show us some affirmation. It is time to rise above being satisfied with half chewed drumsticks and feast on the bounty that Christ, the Good Shepherd, has provided for us in the presence of our enemies.

Paul then says this in the middle of it all;

4 On the contrary, we speak as those approved by God to be entrusted with the gospel. We are not trying to please people but God, who tests our hearts.

What does this verse teach us?

- Our approval already comes from God.
- We must learn to rest in this truth by faith.

Paul wasn't saying he was someone special but that he rested in the truth that his approval to be entrusted with the gospel message came directly from God. He didn't have to force it or manipulate people or trick anyone to get their approval and backing to accomplish his ministry. We are placed in the perfect holy one as a result of his work for us on the cross. When things get tough in your ministry you can remember that in fact it is the ministry of Christ we enter into. He calls us to share in **his ministry** that he began when on earth. When it is tough we must remember that **the responsibility for fruit or "success" rests on the Spirit as our work is to plant and water while God grants the increase.** It is his ministry and he has already approved us to be agents of reconciliation on his behalf.

God daily tests our hearts in order to grow our faith.

- What matters is the inner reality of who we truly are in Christ being lived out in obedience by faith every day.
- For God to test our hearts means that we don't have to prove ourselves to others but constantly keep right before the commander in chief.
- YET....
- The reality is the testing of our hearts is a complete and thorough examination of "fitness" for ministry. It is right that the Holy Spirit examines us daily and his light is extremely bright for he doesn't miss a thing.
- It is a bright shining of the spotlight of the light of the holiness of God into our innermost being. Who among us can endure such intense scrutiny?

Only through the mercy of Christ who gave up his life can we withstand such a holy revelation of what we are really like. Therefore to have God examine our hearts is to daily look to the cross with deep appreciation for the work of Christ on our behalf.

If we are not abiding in Christ by walking in the power of the Holy Spirit our hearts are not right and we need to repent and "grieve, mourn and wail" if needed and get our hearts right. Ministry accomplished with the two sets of false triplets where we seek to manipulate or trick people is human nature and easily done. We don't have to do a course in mask wearing!

To be an authentic person whose approval comes from the Lord is a surrender of all who we are. It often will mean suffering and misunderstanding among other difficulties.

The Church by its very nature as the body of Christ and the family of God must get its approval from God alone. All means that arise from the flesh must be identified and forsaken as a blight on the spotless bride of Christ.

It is all worth it though as this hymn by Robert Robinson reminds us;

>Come Thou fount of every blessing
>**Tune my heart** to sing Thy grace
>Streams of mercy never ceasing
>Call for songs of loudest praise
>
>Teach me some melodious sonnet
>Sung by flaming tongues above
>Praise the mount, I'm fixed upon it
>Mount of Thy redeeming love
>
>Come my Lord, no longer tarry
>Take my ransomed soul away
>Send Thine angels now to carry
>Me to realms of endless days

6

The Family Triplet

The Church is a family
Part 1 CHILD, MOTHER, FATHER
Part 2 ENCOURAGE, COMFORT, WARN

---

1 Thessalonians 2: 6-12

6 We were not looking for praise from people, not from you or anyone else, even though as apostles of Christ we could have asserted our authority. **7 Instead, we were like young children among you. Just as a nursing mother cares for her children, 8** so we cared for you. Because we loved you so much, we were delighted to share with you not only the gospel of God but our lives as well. **9** Surely you remember, brothers and sisters, our toil and hardship; we worked night and day in order not to be a burden to anyone while we preached the gospel of God to you. **10** You are witnesses, and so is God, of how holy, righteous and blameless we were among you who believed. **11** For you know that we dealt with each of you as a father deals with his own children, **12** encouraging, comforting and urging you to live lives worthy of God, who calls you into his kingdom and glory.

PART 1

Paul in this section defends the gospel by defending his own actions. He is being accused of many things and that casts a long shadow on the legitimacy of his message, which is the gospel. He has just cleared the ground of the negative and now plants the positive. In the last chapter we covered the ways that we can do ministry that are inauthentic and end up doing great damage to the kingdom of God. Paul lists these sinful ways in staccato fashion, one after another with minimal explanation. They are not unknown as they are the ways of the world and all of us are very familiar with how the world works. Paul describes in the second half of 1 Thessalonians 2:1-12 how their ministry really was and in so doing has left us a picture of what healthy ministry among new believers really looks like. He does this through the use of three metaphors, one of which is somewhat debated but I do feel the evidence is strong enough to take seriously. A family is made up of a man and a woman and this family is added to when they have children.

Many times I have shared with couples about to be married that they are already a family…they are not a "non-family". Nevertheless children are a natural and rewarding part of family life and are to be valued.

Paul describes his ministry in relational terms or more specifically along family lines. Paul is in essence describing godly leadership principles that can be neglected in the pursuit of authority coupled with the insidious insecurity with which we can be so prone. To walk as a leader who faces their own insecurities is essential yet I have found to do so requires a humility that is a long way from being natural. It is very much a part of dying to self and needs to be faced squarely and repented of. Insecurity always comes from moving away from life in the Spirit so requires a special sensitivity enabling us to be quickly aware when we are operating in the flesh. Scripture has many other leadership or ministry principles and this is only one facet. All the same without this aspect of ministry or leadership we only have the skeleton or the framework.

The real substance of ministry and therefore leadership is strong love which means knowing how to be deeply relational. We must learn to live life with a warm beating heart. To do that we need to get real when our hearts are cold and have spiritually stopped beating.

I wonder how many of our theological colleges and training centres are seriously keeping love as a key ingredient in the lives of our future leaders as they are shaped? It is all too easy to focus on knowledge and results or even performance without the alignment of the heart. The "course" or syllabus for love though can only come from above as Paul prayed;

14... for this reason I bow my knees before the Father, 15from whom every family in heaven and on earth derives its name. 16I ask that out of the riches of His glory He may strengthen you with power through His Spirit in your inner being, 17so that Christ may dwell in your hearts through faith. Then you, being rooted and grounded in love, 18will have power, together with all the saints, to comprehend the length and width and height and depth 19of the love of Christ, and to know this love that surpasses knowledge, that you may be filled with all the fullness of God.[34]

1. We were like infants among you

This is a hotly debated verse though I don't think it really needs to be! It all boils down to the presence or absence of a single Greek letter on the front of the word which can then either mean "gentle" or "infant." The word for infant has an 'v' up front which is similar to the English 'n' yet apart from that they are the same.

Here is a quote from the "Baker Deep End blog";

---

[34] Ephesians 3:14-19

In 1 Thess. 2:7 Paul says either that "we were like little children [Greek = νήπιοι] among you" (NIV) or "we were gentle [Greek = ἤπιοι] among you" (ESV).[35]

Sometimes a choice between various ancient bible manuscripts can be very tricky. So much debate and even division has occurred due to the preference of one manuscript over another. Even the context may not easily settle the matter. I am convinced that the stronger argument is for the retention of the longer word rather than the shorter one. This then means to use "infants" instead of "gentle."

I rather like the translation by respected Thessalonians academic Jeffrey Weima.[36] The rendering then would be ;

"For we never came with a word of flattery (as you know), nor with a motive of greed (God is our witness!) nor were we demanding honor from people, neither from you nor from others (even though we could have insisted on our importance as apostles of Christ), **but we became infants among you**. As a nursing mother cherishes her own children, so we, because we cared so much for you, were pleased to share with you not only the gospel of God but also our own selves, because you became beloved to us."[37]

So if we go with "infants" then the initial issue is what can Paul possibly mean? The fear of saying that Paul thinks we should act like a baby is why I believe most shy away despite the evidence. To describe someone as a child normally means to "pick them up" for not being adult like and able to handle responsibility. Yet even Jesus said that to enter the Kingdom of Heaven we must come as a child. He was using an aspect of being a child that we are supposed to imitate and in many ways not grow out of! I believe Paul is doing the same here. In this context it

---

[35] https://bbhchurchconnection.wordpress.com/
[36] https://bbhchurchconnection.wordpress.com/2014/12/31/was-paul-gentle-or-like-infants-a-closer-look-at-1-thess-27
[37] Weima's translation of 1 Thessalonians 2:5-8

does not mean "immature" or "without capacity to have an opinion" or "baby christians."

Amy Grant released a hilarious song called "fat baby" on one of her early albums. It was a real challenge to us as young people to grow up in Christ and not be stunted in our growth. This is not what this passage is talking about although the words are still great so here is the first bit of the song;

> I know a man, maybe you know him, too
> You never can tell; he might even be you
> He knelt at the altar, and that was the end
> He's saved, and that's all that matters to him
> His spiritual tummy, it can't take too much
> One day a week, he gets a spiritual lunch
> On Sunday, he puts on his spiritual best
> And gives his language a spiritual rest
> He's just a faaa…
> He's just a fat little baby!

Paul was far from being a fat baby. He was a toned spiritual athlete and he longed for everyone else to become spiritually strong as well. His spiritual athleticism is a powerful model for us all. The reference to being like an infant signifies a willingness to not push their apostolic authority too far. Paul does seem to refer to Silas and Timothy as being Apostles as well but that discussion is for another time. To be among them as children was not that they were wanting to just play games or feel they couldn't share the truth because that is exactly what they were doing. It means a humble submissiveness that allowed the Spirit of God to flow through them without the need for force or argument or insisting on obedience which in some cultures especially is a tough call for someone with authority!

To not have a combative spirit is a rare jewel which can be seen to be weak and spineless. When prompted to be like an infant in this sense the power of God will be present and the flow of the Spirit will be felt by all. It is precisely because they have spiritual authority that they can become as gentle and humble as children. I have discovered when I choose to operate in this way when prompted by God that some still can look with disdain on such a posture. That does not in any way mean it was wrong of me to do so. To operate in the Spirit will frequently bring misunderstanding, judgement and even condemnation. We have a role model in our saviour who endured such treatment frequently while on earth.

2. We were like a nursing mother among you

Just as a nursing mother cares for her children, **8** so we **cared** for you. Because we **loved** you so much, we were delighted to **share** with you not only the gospel of God but our lives as well.

So here we have three men who were like nursing mothers as well as little children among the new converts… how does this sit with our Alpha males !!

It teaches us something about true masculinity. To be masculine as a man and to be feminine as a woman is a deep submission to the plan of God who created "…them male and female." If we have "gender doubts" about who we are and do not seek the word of God for the answers we will continue to have deep struggles throughout life. The amazing thing is that our creator knows why we might feel a certain way about ourselves and can guide us into his perfect will no matter how hard and bumpy and circuitous it might be. He does not "write us off" even when others do. He journeys the road with us and will bring transformation if we seek his will with an honest heart. The church must be open to the journey aspect of maturity and not insist that we all arrive at the same point at the same time.

A man according to the word of God is strong and not easily pushed around. While 1 Corinthians 16:13 could be translated in a variety of ways the most natural way to translate 'ἀνδρίζομαι' (andrizomai) is probably 'to be strong like a man'.[38] A man stands up for what he believes in and is committed to carving out a path in life with diligence and endurance with real patience. Yet a man is also called upon to "… not be harsh" with his wife and to display compassion creativity and gentleness. This way of being does not make him any less of a man. So for these three men, why be like a mother, specifically a nursing mother? The idea is described in the Greek verb translated "cared." They "cared" for the Thessalonians like a nursing mother. The Greek word θάλπω (Thalpo) according to Strong's concordance has the idea of keeping another person warm, of not leaving someone else cold or destitute. It also means to draw close to someone, to not pull away from them, even if what we see we don't always like. This important Greek word includes the idea of choosing to value someone dearly. Hence we get the old word "cherish" which has the idea of considering someone of great value. Instead of considering them as being worthless we instead practically demonstrate that they are worthy of our time and sacrifice. This also helps us to see that the role of a mother is to deeply value her own children and for them to know how treasured they are. This doesn't mean they are pampered or allowed to do what they want. The truth is if we didn't "…. train up our children in the way they should go"[39] It would indicate they were not valued.

In considering ministry among any group of people we are to demonstrate to them just how much God cherishes them by daily reaching out and warming them with the love we receive from Christ himself. Leaders in the church and all of us as the body of Christ are called to

---

[38] 1 Corinthians 16:13 Be on the alert. Stand firm in the faith. Be men of courage. Be strong

[39] Proverbs 22:6 Train up a child in the way he should go, and when he is old he will not depart from it.

not leave each other out in the cold. This is a graphic and even heartbreaking image of what can all too easily be done at times. To avoid this we need to stay close to Christ so he can warm our hearts when they are becoming stony, frigid or even begin to melt with fear. When we are close to Christ he reveals the needs of others to our spirits so we can be as Christ to them.

3. We dealt with each of you as a Father

11 For you know that we dealt with each of you **as a father deals** with his own children, **12** encouraging, comforting and urging you to live lives worthy of God, who calls you into his kingdom and glory.

On Father's Day we place our focus on the Dads. Some might say every day is Father's day! Some single dads though who are either not allowed to see their kids or severely restricted for whatever reason would definitely not feel that any day of the year is their day.

This third aspect of the family triplet is for everyone though.

We are going to see how important this family triplet is for effective ministry. Maybe we are inclined in the right sense to be like an infant or like a mother or like a father or none of these yet the word of God calls us to display all such characteristics or at least intentionally begin to live out such roles. The reality is we need to embrace all three leadership dimensions.

What is the significance of what Paul might mean when he says we are to lead as fathers? Thankfully he explains it otherwise we might be inclined to just bring our own ideas to this verse and all sorts of problems might eventuate. The most striking thing about the three verbs that Paul uses to describe how they were like a Father to the Thessalonians is they all fit into one type of activity. It might not be what we tend to expect when talking about the role of Fathers. Firstly, before we launch into this passage, despite where society seems to be floating at the moment, it is certainly right to consider a Father to be a protector and provider.

Protectors and providers

Fathers can be culturally considered to be protectors and providers and this is certainly also taught in Scripture. For a man to not be bothered doing either of these two activities would be very neglectful as a father and might even prove that they do not really care for anyone but themselves. A hard working protector and provider of their family is what a good Dad is. Given this we can actually presume that these two are already in operation now as we proceed to a third area which Paul sees as fundamental and even a priority. This third area and the only one addressed in this chapter is the call to be a communicator.

A Father is to be able to speak into the lives of his children and not leave it to the "boss" or the "spiritual one" in other words his wife! If you are an Aussie you would be very familiar with these terms and understandings of our wives. We might even laugh yet there are issues with such ways of referring to our spouses even if it is done in jest. The least of these is the surrender of our responsibility to be a spiritual leader and leaving such things to "the missus" as is commonly done in the Great South Land. If a man is to be a communicator and not just a doer then why do many blokes find it so hard? That is a very big question and there are probably a whole host of cultural and spiritual answers. Lurking behind all of this though is an archenemy who does not want men to take any true responsibility in the church or the family as this would bring a sense of spiritual order and release power that Satan does not want to see. As you read this please do not hear that women are not as spiritual as men or as gifted. In fact one of the reasons that many Aussie men hand over spiritual responsibility to their wives is out of their sense of spiritual inferiority. They often see the church women including their own wives as being more spiritually articulate and more administrative so they are happy to let them "run the show" and undertake most of the leadership. The current gender climate while addressing some necessary imbalances has also caused men to be less inclined to put up their hand for certain roles as they might have done in years past. Just what then is the way out of having shirked spiritual responsibility for many years? We'll get to that but the short answer lies in Romans 1:5 which refers to "…the obedience that comes from faith." Choose by faith to do what is not easy and your faith muscle will grow. Choose by faith to work through why you might have left everything to the ladies and learn to humbly stand up and follow Christ while also not becoming harsh and overbearing.

PART 2 How to be a Father in ministry

We now move into the second triplet grouping. Here we discover the three ways that Paul described their "Father" ministry among them. He is keen to see healthy leadership flourishing in the crucial area of communication. A leader who is poor in aspects of communication will always struggle no matter what other capacities they might possess.

To be like a Father among those we serve we must be spiritual communicators from the heart.

Let's look at the three ways we can do this.

1. ENCOURAGE

Parakaleo.   **Greek: παρακαλέω**

    This special term which is also used for the Spirit's work means literally to come alongside and call or speak into their lives. This is not done from some kind of intellectual, physical or spiritual distance or high place. We cannot be "six foot above contradiction" as ministers who preached from a very high pulpit (maybe with eagles wings off to the side) and who did not mingle with the common people were said to be like. It is translated as "to encourage or to exhort or beseech" or even to "admonish or console or comfort."

This is clearly an important verb which Paul also used when writing to the Corinthians;

Finally, brothers and sisters, rejoice! Strive for full restoration, **encourage one another**, be of one mind, live in peace. And the God of love and peace will be with you.[40]

One of the ways this verb is used is in "direct encouragement." When we are discouraged we lack the heart to "...get back on the horse." We no longer desire to or believe we can do something we used to be able to do or were committed to achieving. Sadly it is all too easy as we become older to progressively feel that way. We need our spiritual armour on to resist such an attack by the enemy of our souls. The truth is physical capacity has no correlation with spiritual prowess. We can be very broken and weak in our bodies yet be running at a great pace and even flying in the thermals if we live by faith in Christ. To be discouraged is to no longer have the boldness, the fearlessness and the imperative to be who we are called to be. It is to no longer have the desire or energy to walk according to our calling in Christ. Remember Paul's words to Timothy reminding him that we have not been given a spirit of timidity but of power, love and a sound mind? With mental illness on the rise this mention here of a sound mind deserves some closer attention!

Here is the same verse in two different versions;

12 **encouraging**, comforting and urging you to live lives worthy of God, who calls you into his kingdom and glory. NIV

---

[40] 2 Corinthians 13:11

12 we exhorted each one of you **and encouraged you** and charged you to walk in a manner worthy of God, who calls you into his own kingdom and glory. ESV

This verb then, this dimension of Fatherhood is used when the child, adult or church is discouraged and has lost a sense of hope. What might this encouragement then look like?

- To animate through words
- To believe in and declare it to the person
- To spur someone on to persevering in what they are called to be and do in Christ
- To speak positively where negative things have been said over them
- To lift up when down
- To fire someone up

2. Comfort

Paramutheomai. Greek: παραμυθέομαι

This Greek word has the idea of speaking in a soothing way by coming close to the person. It is a compound word that combines the term for "close beside" with the word for "soothing speaking."

The idea then is to come close to the child or person and to speak gentle, soothing words that bring comfort. The same word is used when Martha and Mary were comforted by those present with soothing words when Lazarus died. To use soothing words and not harsh or distant words or careless or selfish words is the call of a father. A father has to be tough at times yet we are told clearly in Scripture to never be harsh and there is a big difference. A father who communicates from the heart knows when to drop tools, leave what they had prioritised and come close with the intention of listening to his children whom he loves dearly. They know how to offer the soothing words that are needed. Therefore this second activity of a biological father with our children and a spiritual father with those we minister among is to cry out to God for the wisdom to be able to come close and speak soothing words to those in pain. It is especially used when our children both spiritual and biological or adopted are clearly suffering. What does this exactly look like?

What are we called to do to accomplish such a crucial means of loving those to whom we are fathers? Here is a practical list of ideas to stimulate our thinking and activity in this area;

- To leave what we are doing
- To focus on the person
- To hear their pain
- To speak soothing words…like honey
- To be patient once those words are spoken
- To adjust our words so healing takes place

This is the role of a father. It is a long way from a harsh authority that terrifies a child into submission. It is also a call to be warm and connected no matter what our own upbringing may have conditioned us to believe and to act.

3. Warn

Marturomai Greek: **Greek: μαρτύρομαι**

This multi-faceted Greek word includes the elements of testifying as a witness as well as affirming and warning someone about something to the point of strong protest.

This is a particularly strong word that is used with a measure of risk, hence a witness who loses their life by speaking out is a "martyr".

Paul uses this verb in **Ephesians 4:17**

So I tell you this, and **INSIST** (Marturomai) on it in the Lord, that you must no longer live as the Gentiles do, in the futility of their thinking.

The idea conveyed here is one of a "strong insistence coupled with a warning of the consequences." Some versions stay "I charge you" in other words I direct you to do "such and such." When Paul was speaking to the Ephesians he was very concerned they might go off the track and return to their old ways so he used this word... I insist...I charge...I cannot state more strongly. The idea is someone "getting tough on someone else" by not really giving them a choice.

The person is saying;

"This is really the only way as any other way and things are going to fall apart! Don't mess your life up!"

We believe in them so much that we can't just let them fall into the devil's trap. I "testify to" means I make it very clear and refuse to gloss over the facts of the matter. It means I bring the matter out into the very bright light. A coach at half time might be described as doing this if his team has some sloppy habits creeping back in!

> *STOP THE RUBBISH... ! I'm not going to pretend I didn't see what was going on...look around... don't kick randomly... Look for the man leading...handball when needed... don't get caught with the ball...do you even want to win?*

It is used when our children/ministry family are in grave danger spiritually or otherwise. The idea is to invade their space even when they don't want it!

- To get them uncomfortable... creating a risky situation for the father
- To dispel the fog of apathy ... or outright pigheadedness
- To wake up... to danger...to open up their eyes
- To warn against something
- To point toward the truth that may be hard to swallow

When referring to leadership this dimension would have to be saved up for those occasions when a tough word was needed and there was the clear leading of the Spirit. If harsh and critical ways of leading are regularly employed then when this dimension does need to be employed there will be little to no "buy in" by the team or body of believers. To "insist"on something in today's climate of "leadership being earned not given" means that it has to be used sparingly and thoughtfully. On the other hand if we are "spineless" in our leadership then we might never move to being someone who ever insists on anything and so the "church ship" is tossed by the waves of opinion and disharmony.

For the church to operate effectively we need to be as humble as children by not demanding our rights, as caring as mothers by warmly drawing close to others and being strong communicators as Fathers as we speak into the lives of others.

7
The Intercessory Triplet

The Church never stops its intercessory work
WAYMAKER, LOVE CREATOR, HEART STRENGTHENER

---

1 Thessalonians 3:11-13

11 Now may our God and Father himself and our Lord Jesus clear the way for us to come to you. 12 May the Lord make your love increase and overflow for each other and for everyone else, just as ours does for you. 13 May he strengthen your hearts so that you will be blameless and holy in the presence of our God and Father when our Lord Jesus comes with all his holy ones.

Introduction and context

It is abundantly obvious that the "Apostolic Triplet Team" have a strong affection for this new church. The Triplet ministry team does not have the motto of "teach and disappear" or "save and drop in the deep end." They are committed to them as people. They are committed to their growth and their protection and their complete spiritual development.

They are more than scalps or servants or projects and they certainly are not numbers to add to their missionary tally.

They are fellow members of the Royal Family! The evil one is out to destroy them and the Triplet team know this and are deeply concerned about it. They sent Timothy to just see how they were all going. Firstly Paul was determined to see if knowledge of their trials had unsettled them. In other words had these difficulties made them feel like God had deserted them or that they were not on the right path because things were so tough for the ones who were discipling them. Maybe this "travelling trio" were not true teachers? Maybe God was punishing them?

He lets them know that they were destined for suffering, that it is "part and parcel" of the life of anyone who wants to follow Christ in a world that is "hellbent" on going its own way. The world hates being told to repent and runs from asking for forgiveness for what it loves to do. That is when Paul says the following;

I was afraid that in some way the tempter had tempted you and that our labours might have been in vain. 1 Thessalonians 3:5

Paul is acutely aware of the work of the tempter, the deceiver, the enemy of our souls "tricking us" by presenting candy coated sin. He knows that the ancient serpent will just "out and out" lie about the reality of who God is and how the Christian life works by always giving us "attractive alternatives" that are inherently broken.

He describes it in such strong terms... *"that our labours might have been in vain..."* despite all the good.

Firstly it is clear from all of this that we can fall to such a low position where we are no longer able to serve God in his kingdom. In fact we can end up working for the enemy despite all the progress we might have made. This is a grim warning and a strong call to make sure we put on our armour daily. It is a trumpet blast to make sure we live by faith and fight the enemy. It is a summons to live for Christ and to live for eternity. We can't just take big long holidays from being a soldier in the Lord's army as this effectively means we end up going AWOL[41] or worse joining the other team.

Secondly the effort and faith steps and suffering that our spiritual leaders, mentors and teachers put in can "go down the gurgler."

That is such a serious and even horrific situation to be in. Is it really the case that we rob our christian "fathers and mothers" of joy and delight and even their very work when we fail to grow and give in to temptation and allow evil to return? YES! Paul is even speaking like we invalidate the work done when we turn away and fail to grow. All this is not to pour guilt upon us but to spur us on to healthy commitment and maturity. He is speaking to the church after all, not speaking at a conference or just writing a book about ministry.

A note of clarification

The big truth is God rewards our faithfulness with or without results. He has seen our work whether it is received, believed and absorbed or not and he will reward us. Just think of the call that Isaiah received. He was to preach his message until the following occurred;
"Until the cities lie ruined
    and without inhabitant,
until the houses are left deserted
    and the fields ruined and ravaged,
12
until the Lord has sent everyone far away
    and the land is utterly forsaken. [42]

---

[41] Absent With Out Leave...military term...common use today to mean "off doing what we want to do without any regard for others or our leaders or our mentors."

[42] Isaiah 6:11-12

God calls us to obedience which means leaving the results up to him. Here in this verse we are taught the other side of the coin. We must remember to always hold biblical truths in tension or we will be pulled "here and there" and never gain perspective. This is far more important than many realise. Let's "take a gander"[43] at an Aussie analogy. We have sadly heard various forms of the following scenario too many times in the last few years. Some amazing family (they all have names…and faces…and lives) spends 14 years (or more) lovingly building the house of their dreams in the bush. They had collected special little pieces of wood and every room and wall was tenderly finished off when time and money was available. Then the unthinkable happens, an intense bushfire sweeps through and everything is lost, even the landscaped gardens, the orchard, the sheds, the tanks…all gone.

Was their dedication, creativity and labour all in vain? On one level they learnt a lot. All the shared lessons and experiences were valuable and no lives were lost. There are so many memories and no-one can rob the family of them. The house though is truly gone, the building was in vain. It was unique and done at a time when the family was together and all pitched in. It can never be replaced, there is a grief beyond measure. This is what Paul is talking about…Maturity really matters. What Paul is most worried about is the growth of the life of Christ in this new Church. He didn't want that to be invalidated. He didn't want his spiritual work of being a gardener, a father, and a builder to be in vain. All the more reason why he is regularly checking on his fledgling flock. This is not out of a personal sense of ego but out of a real worry that the evil one might have contaminated their witness, their lives and their faith. It was then that Timothy returned and gave a glowing report of their faith and love. What amazing timing our Lord has and what compassion he has for each one of us. It is worth mentioning that Timothy didn't give the statistics as to how many people they had going to their

---

[43] Let's have a good look… stretch your neck to see better…Aussie slang!

church, reflections on their new building programme or even the number of baptisms! The ministry triplet team are subsequently overjoyed and they even say the following;

8 For **now we really live**, since you are standing firm in the Lord.

We learn so much in this little epistle about where to put our energies, our focus and even what church really is!

The Intercessory Triplet

1 Thessalonians 3:11-13

11 Now may our God and Father himself and our Lord Jesus clear the way for us to come to you. 12 May the Lord make your love increase and overflow for each other and for everyone else, just as ours does for you. 13 May he strengthen your hearts so that you will be blameless and holy in the presence of our God and Father when our Lord Jesus comes with all his holy ones.

This section of the letter is very much worded like a prayer. Certainly Paul would have been praying along these lines. When we come across the word "may" as in "...Now **MAY** our God and Father..." it does not indicate any sense of doubt. It is a way of praying that recognises that without the power of Almighty God things do not change. We cannot expect to see good things happen on our own. It is a way of allowing the King of Kings to be sovereign yet by faith look to him to work. "May...!" or "Let it be..." We beseech you and you alone Oh Almighty God and refuse to look elsewhere for help.

There is strong Trinitarian teaching here also. Our God is one yet distinct. We see here also that Jesus is LORD. He is the one who has the power to make your love increase and also do many other things. It is now time to examine the triplet for intercessory prayer in this passage.

Firstly... WAYMAKER

11 Now may our God and Father himself and our Lord Jesus **clear the way** for us to come to you.

Clear the way, remove the obstacles, open the gates, swing wide the doors! Make the rough ways smooth, fill in every valley, level every hill!

This reveals to us so much about the character of God, just who he declares himself to be and what he wants us to know about himself. He declares himself to be, quite literally, the one who does the impossible!

Remember Mary's words? "how can this be... I am a virgin?"

35 The angel replied, "The Holy Spirit will come upon you, and the power of the Most High will overshadow you. So the Holy One to be born will be called the Son of God. 36Look, even Elizabeth your relative has conceived a son in her old age, and she who was called barren is in her sixth month. **37 For no word from God will ever fail."**[44]

The promise is always that no word from God will ever fail. We do have to learn to make the promises of God our own though. We cannot just leave them in the Bible! We can't just sing about the power of God and then live powerless lives. God is not pleased with a "words only" type of faith. If I say that God is Almighty yet live a powerless life then I am declaring with my actions that God is weak and fickle and unable to act! To an unbeliever our God is as strong as the life we live out in front of them. What a challenging and wonderful thought that is, yet it is the truth. Our lives must match who we declare God to be as his life is only discovered by others through our fleshing out of the life of Christ to a mocking yet desperate world. As the "Give thanks" song declares "and now let the weak say they are strong." **We can't just "defend" the nature of God while refusing to embrace the**

---

[44] Luke 1:35-37

reality of his power in our own lives. When we do that we are being cultural fundamentalists rather than faith walking, Spirit filled believers and there is a big difference. The former defends what we have been raised to believe without any need to embrace the life of Christ who is the vine. The latter enters personally into the life of the vine by choosing to "abide" every day. We must declare the reality of God with active love and power and back it up with words. An angry defence and righteous indignation of wickedness in the world on its own will usually not tend to be the means of people coming to Christ. A common fallback though is to denounce the sins of the world in an even stronger way as we discover how ugly our own lives are. This somehow makes us feel we are still following Christ despite the wickedness of our own hearts. Paul is being honest by saying the way really is blocked. He pours out his heart to God for a way to be opened up. He also pours out his heart to the church about his affection and sadness of not being able to see them personally. **Intercession will often include facing a blocked highway filled with rubble and earnestly praying on behalf of another for this intimidating pile to be taken out of the way.** We must intercede for each other and not just petition God for our own needs.

Secondly .... LOVE CREATOR

12 May the Lord make **your love increase and overflow** for each other and for everyone else, just as ours does for you.

The Thessalonian church already demonstrated a considerable degree of warm connection. There is real care among them yet things can block a deeper love. The Spirit through Paul is saying to not let natural limits, objections and distance keep us from a holy and full love for each other. In other words despite our natural tendencies, limited viewpoints and past hurts we must not put a cap on love! It is a call that reflects the agape love of the Father.

It is all too easy in some regards to enjoy being part of a church family and loving the glow we get from hanging around with caring people. If not done by faith and in the Spirit's power though it becomes a "natural" attempt to do what is only possible through the Spirit of God. There is a limit to a human generated community which is an attempt to establish what only the Spirit of God through born again believers can truly accomplish.

COMMUNITY

For centuries human beings have attempted to create **communities** of many kinds as we all know how important such a way of living is. The world and the church are always talking about it. It is such a buzz word that pastors and community leaders alike use it frequently as they know that it is deep within the hearts of us all. We know we are designed for it and people who live on their own or without connection to each other are either seriously wounded or will deteriorate mentally and miss out on so much. Clubs and communes seek to gather "likeminded" people together to form a group that believes in a common goal and are willing to follow certain rules and show compassion for each other. This is a common expression of community. Unfortunately such attempts at group formation can fail though as there are limits to our capacity to form a viable community. These limits are "sinful human" limits which can only be truly removed in Christ.

The memories of the attempt to cultivate some form of community though can be the best memories of our lives because even the attempt itself sparked off all sorts of deep things of the heart. On the other hand those memories can be filled with pain as sinful practices may have surfaced and ugly blotches of human nature revealed themselves causing real trauma. Paul is calling God's people first of all to be filled with the love of God at all times by being filled with the Spirit. Only then can we attempt to make community a serious proposition. Hence there is the need for us all to be people who "...pray without ceasing" as only in a prayer drenched atmosphere can true Christian community thrive. Without the framework of scripture and the power of the Spirit we cannot love each other in the way that Paul encourages the Thessalonians to pursue. Love, we must recall is an act of faith, not of feelings. We love because we have been loved first by the lover of our souls and his love is constant and without "key performance indicators!" Jesus tells us to love the unlovely and he words it this way... "Whatsoever you do ...unto the least of these my brothers...you do unto me."

40 "The King will reply, 'Truly I tell you, whatever you did for one of the least of these brothers and sisters of mine, you did for me.'[45]

Here is part of the secret, the secret to a "filled up life", to being a growing individual in the midst of a community;

Loving others with God's love as unto Christ...

Human nature tends to either be;

- Snobbish... keep the riff raff out!
- Sensitive... we are hurt by every word said or not said
- Solitary...acting as if we don't need others
- Suspicious...looking for ulterior motives
- Superior... enduring the ways of lesser mortals
- Stuck... unable to mature and leave behind past hurts.

Whatever our issue, our weakness or our tendency, in Christ **we can lay it down.** The Superior can then be humble, the Snobbish can move freely among other levels of society, the Stuck can be free. We then discover that as Jesus was and is so are we and authentic community begins.

---

[45] Matthew 25:40

The biblical word is fellowship which despite its old fashioned sound is truly a beautiful thing as it is the fruit of deep spiritual unity given to us through the work of Christ. Intercession then will include praying along these lines. Praying that love might increase, that our hearts will be as one and that there will be genuine affection.

Thirdly… Heart Strengthener

13 May he **strengthen your hearts** so that you will be blameless and holy in the presence of our God and Father when our Lord Jesus comes with all his holy ones.

Our natural physical hearts can be wounded and become weak. Physical hearts can become damaged and not able to function with the capacity they used to be able to do. There are so many causes of heart wounding in the natural just as there are in the spiritual. Satan is out to wound our hearts and he is a specialist as he is a heart destroyer. But just as we have seen for the other two areas, we cannot make these three aspects just about ourselves as this is about intercession for others. When we pray for others to have their hearts strengthened we make our own hearts stronger. Let's examine what might cause hearts to be wounded. In the natural there are many causes of heart problems;

- Disease,
- Thin walls
- Holes in the heart
- lifestyle choices such as drugs and lack of rest
- Genetic weakness and many more

How can our hearts also be wounded in the spiritual realm?

The short answer is by SIN and SUFFERING. Here are some examples;

- Betrayal
- Relationship breakdown
- Abuse of many kinds
- Discouraging words spoken by us or over us
- Having the "rug swept out from under us" when we get close to achieving something
- Not choosing wisely
- Extreme guilt over sinful practices
- Suffering and persecution…trials…ours and others

So many things can cause us to "lose heart" and give up. All of this can be in order to protect our weak and vulnerable or guilty hearts. Remember this is about intercession which is how to pray for others. When we notice the following **symptoms** of a weakened heart in a fellow believer we are called to pray and intercede for them;

- fear
- pushing others away
- disengagement
- temper tantrums
- control issues
- inability to see the positive
- sadness
- constant weeping
- depression

We must pray for them to get stronger hearts. We must intercede for them to be able to live "blameless and holy lives" right through to the appearing of Christ. Our goal also must be personal maturity which means living out what we pray for in others. Can God strengthen damaged and wounded hearts? Can he heal broken hearts?

Hear the words of Psalm 147;

> Praise the Lord. How good it is to sing praises to our God, how pleasant and fitting to praise him! 2 The Lord builds up Jerusalem; he gathers the exiles of Israel. 3 He heals the brokenhearted and binds up their wounds. 4 He determines the number of the stars and calls them each by name. 5 Great is our Lord and mighty in power; his understanding has no limit. 6 The Lord sustains the humble but casts the wicked to the ground.

He can only heal our wounded hearts if we want to get strong. Remember Jesus interaction with the man who was unable to walk?

> 5 One man there had been an invalid for thirty-eight years. 6 When Jesus saw him lying there and realized that he had spent a long time in this condition, He asked him, **"Do you want to get well?"** [46]

Why on earth would the King of Hearts ask such a question? It sounds callous and insensitive yet there are certain advantages to staying weak. What might they be?

- Self pity
- Laziness
- We don't have to "spring" out of bed in the morning
- lack of responsibility
- People checking up on us
- Good excuse to not get too involved

Once we are strong we wish we had not waited so long. It feels so good to have a strong and fearless heart! To be able to take on the world

---

[46] John 5:5,6

through faith in this Almighty God we serve and who lives in us by his Spirit.

A healthy church will be thoroughly committed to intercession in order for roadblocks to be cleared, for love to abound and for hearts to be strong. This intercession will be biblical, heartfelt and sacrificial.

8

The Purity Triplet

The Church is an Exclusive lover
**AVOID IMPURITY, SHOW SELF CONTROL,
DON'T TAKE ADVANTAGE**

---

1 Thessalonians 4:1-8

4 As for other matters, brothers and sisters, we instructed you how to live in order to please God, as in fact you are living. Now we ask you and urge you in the Lord Jesus to do this more and more. **2** For you know what instructions we gave you by the authority of the Lord Jesus. **3** It is God's will that you should be sanctified: that you should **avoid sexual immorality; 4** that each of you should learn to **control your own body** in a way that is holy and honourable, **5** not in passionate lust like the pagans, who do not know God; **6** and that in this matter **no one should wrong or take advantage of a brother or sister.** The Lord will punish all those who commit such sins, as we told you and warned you before. **7** For God did not call us to be impure, but to live a holy life. **8** Therefore, anyone who rejects this instruction does not reject a human being but God, the very God who gives you his Holy Spirit.

Introduction

It is time to talk seriously about our sexuality and not just leave this area to unregulated social media and to the peers of our children! The big truth is we are created physical, intellectual, emotional, and relational yet also sexual. We grow in our understanding of the former four dimensions from a very young age while the powerful latter reality is somewhat thrust upon at puberty. Our sexual awareness is deliberately reserved for a later time. It is awakened within us as we mature as the lover in the Song of Solomon so poetically describes;

Daughters of Jerusalem, I charge you
    by the gazelles and by the does of the field:
Do not arouse or awaken love
    until it so desires.[47]

All in all this sexual awakening is ultimately a preparation for exclusive marriage which is not to be selfishly used prior to a wedding covenant. Our sexuality is a precious gift, yet as we all know it is inherent with issues in our brokenness. It truly is an incredibly potent force for good or for evil. Some appear to blame all erotic experimentation on the "sexual revolution of the 1960's" as if all was perfect prior to that time period. The reality however is the explosive capacity of our sexual chemistry has always been capable of great power which has needed to be appropriately channeled. The bible is full of stories where this unbridled force has led to great destruction.[48] God in his wisdom has given this special gift to us. It has an immediate physical and emotional purpose which we can readily acknowledge and participate in when the

---

[47] Song of Solomon 2:7. This verse can of course be interpreted as not hurrying romantic love in a growing adult relationship. It is also right to not expect a child to feel what only a sexually mature person is supposed to feel.

[48] The story of Amnon and Tamar in 2 Samuel 13 is just one of many such accounts where the results were devastating.

time is right. The gift of our sexuality also goes beyond the temporal and is supposed to teach us deep spiritual truths for our edification. Our sexuality and the deep need for emotional and eventually spiritual intimacy are strongly connected though perhaps in ways we might not fully understand.

Paul kicks off this section by positively acknowledging the growth of the Thessalonians and then he quickly moves to insisting that this growth must not stop! He in essence says for them to keep on keeping on, to keep on growing and to keep on maturing. We as the hearers of this letter could all too rapidly get offended at this point believing we are actually doing quite well yet that is the very thing that will block any further growth. It is important that there is no break in our spiritual growth as stagnation can quickly cause moral decline. We must seek to grow more and more in order to not accept a level of "having arrived." Only as we strive forward can we overcome lethargy and apathy. The purpose set out in this passage is a call to live in a way that pleases God. It is true we are forever acceptable in Christ, yet we are saved to please his heart through our obedient faithful lives. This is the "Grace & Holiness" tension which must never be relaxed until we are promoted to glory. John captures this thought in the third chapter of his first letter;

> 21Beloved, if our hearts do not condemn us, we have confidence before God, 22and we will receive from Him whatever we ask, because we keep His commandments and **do what is pleasing in His sight.**[49]

This "command" with Christ's authority at the beginning of chapter 4 of 1 Thessalonians is after 3 chapters of affection, grace and faith. It is not at the beginning of the letter. The branching actions of the tree of our lives must flow from a healthy trunk and extensive root system which Paul has carefully laid out in the first 3 chapters. Historically we as "the church" have been known for our strong stand against sex-

---

[49] 1 John 3:21-22

ual sin to the point where "sex" itself is characterised as something to be avoided or even be ashamed about. Conversely another church can be known for their "tolerance" of all things no matter what and take pride in what they permit and allow despite what the word of God says. Different churches can land in very different places in these matters. How difficult yet how crucial it is to be people who embrace the whole of Scripture.

Here is the word of God;

"It is God's will that you should be sanctified" 1 Thess 4:3a

THE WILL OF GOD

Learning to live for the will of God requires the surrender of our will to him. Our soul is made up of our mind, our emotions and a neglected powerful component called the will. We truly do have the potential to choose one way or another. We are not instinctual as we have wills that can say yes or no to any inner impulses. This aspect of being made in the image of God is what sets us apart from all other creatures. The fact that something has truly gone awry in this dimension though is a truth that cannot be ignored. We must ask ourselves why we choose so quickly what is spiritually harmful ?

Part of the answer is expressed in the following Proverb;

Trust in the lord with all your heart and lean not on your own understanding...[50]

How crucial it is to not "lean on our own understanding." Whenever we do so we can make faulty choices due to the inner blindness that we possess. Let's examine the key word in the passage;

---

[50] Proverbs 3:5

Sanctified = Hagiasmos in Greek. To be sanctified (hagiasmos) is a Greek word meaning to be consecrated, purifed and set apart to be holy.

- The process of becoming more like Christ
- The process of growing in holiness

Here we have another clue as to what the church is !

The Church is set apart for a special work determined by God.
Being distinct and different therefore is a vital part of being holy.

Hence **CHURCH** cannot follow a **"full on seeker sensitive approach"** if the purpose is to remove all distinct and different practices. If this is done in order to bring the world in and not be offended, dismayed or frightened we miss the incredible wonder of a divine encounter! The fear of God is a crucial element of being the fellowship of the saints and of being in worship. We can expect "non-natural" things to occur and also expect the Pharisee to be offended!

Remember in the early church where great fear gripped the people and no-one else dared join after Ananias and Sapphira lost their lives by lying to the Holy Spirit. We subsequently read in the very next verse;

"Nevertheless, more and more men and women believed in the Lord and were added to their number."[51]

Hence **EVANGELISM** cannot follow a **"let's become like them to win them" approach.** In the late 1960's and early 1970's there was a **radical evangelism** concept known as **Flirty Fishing**[52] that became popular. David Berg was a leading proponent and this is a a quote from the website bearing his name;

---

[51] Acts 5:14
[52] davidberg.com "The history and theological premise of flirty fishing."

David proposed that the boundaries of expressing God's love to others could at times go beyond just showing kindness and doing good deeds. He suggested that for those who were in dire need of physical love and affection, even sex could serve as evidence to them of God's love.

When we are no longer distinct as a church we neglect holiness. We then seek to reach people for Christ yet without Christ and without his Spirit. No wonder we might struggle sometimes as a church. Becoming HOLY is the most important and crucial and delightful thing you will ever do. When we can do it together we are being the church.

We shall discover soon that holiness and intimacy are strongly linked. Without holiness no-one will see the Lord, just have a look at Hebrews 12:14;

Make every effort to live in peace with everyone and to be holy; **without holiness no one will see the Lord.**

We must ask some questions here....

"How is this to be done?"

"What is getting in the way of this process?"

"How do I prioritise this holiness goal?"

The answer will be **the world, the flesh and the devil,** in many subtle and deceptive ways. We can find ourselves taking pride in our "supposed freedom" to not be holy, to stubbornly refuse to be made like Jesus Christ, to resist being set apart for a holy purpose when it interferes with my agenda and the list goes on.

Just what does this process of sanctification look like?
Three areas

1. That you should avoid sexual immorality

2. That you should control your own body
3. That you should not do wrong to a brother or sister

Why does the Holy Spirit choose the area of sexuality? Why did Paul not talk about theft or covetousness or jealousy or gossip? It does include all those areas as other parts of Scripture teach yet sexual intimacy is a deep well. It is also symbolic of our intimacy with Christ as it points to faithfulness, to holiness, to being one flesh, one body and even unity with God himself. It is about "the power of exclusivity" and just how much Satan attacks such an idea. He will pound us with a thousand ways to be unfaithful to Christ and he will especially use the way we relate sexually as it immediately has a profound spiritual impact.

We are relational beings as well as sexual beings which means we long for union with another human being and that can get pretty intense at times. It may be through a deep loneliness or an overwhelming sense for the need to connect physically or emotionally. That's why when we follow the ways of the world instead of Christ it is called adultery and not just an "affair" or "meandering" onto the wrong path. The popular country song by Barbara Mandrell and David Houston that includes the line "how can this be wrong when it feels so right?" does not help and actually does a world of damage. It is damaging both at an inner personal core level and also beyond with a huge community ripple effect. To use the current terminology it produces a "moral injury" that cannot be pushed easily away. A true understanding of the nature of God is extremely important for our spiritual health. God is not mean to make us sexual beings and then to put a whole package of parameters around our sexual expression.

A journey back in time to the old covenant.

Leviticus 18.

Leviticus was given as part of the holy and righteous law of God under a covenant that is now obsolete. It does continue to point us to holiness though as each aspect is described as **detestable** before the Lord and he does not change. Even New Covenant believers cannot disregard what was abhorrent to Christ under a former covenant as He is the same yesterday, today and forever.

Basically the faithful union of a married man and woman as being the only context for sexual expression is spelt out very clearly in this book of Moses as well as under the new covenant.

Do not be like the Nation you were enslaved to... Egypt... and do not be like the nations that you will possess the land from... the Canaanites, Hivites...etc... [53]

There is a specific Hebrew term in Leviticus for the command "Do not commit sexual immorality" or "do not be sexually intimate with."

The Hebrew word is quite literally... **"do not uncover the nakedness of."** [54] These bible versions below capture the literal sense of the term;

New American Standard Bible
'None of you shall approach any blood relative of his to **uncover nakedness**; I am the LORD.

Douay-Rheims Bible
No man shall approach to her that is near of kin to him, **to uncover her nakedness**. I am the Lord.

---

[53] Leviticus 18:3 states this clearly. *3 You must not do as they do in Egypt, where you used to live, and you must not do as they do in the land of Canaan, where I am bringing you. Do not follow their practices.*

[54] Leviticus 18:6

There are so many applications of this very confronting command from pornography to what we watch on our screens and devices, to how we dress and so much more. Uncovering nakedness if either done to us or done to ourselves or done to others or delighted in vicariously is sexual immorality and moves us away from holiness. Holiness being that joyful faithfulness and commitment to be like Christ with his power that honours him.

Immorality moves us away from holy exclusivity which is at the heart of following a holy God. This is the only time when we can truly use the term **"jealousy"** because as human beings jealousy has so many broken and damaged areas to it but this is not the case with God. He is rightly a **"jealous God"** meaning he longs for an exclusive relationship with us and damage is done when we break this unique connection. This chapter outlines a whole host of wrong sexual liaisons. The list is long and even appears to repeat the same ideas from another angle at times, just to make sure we get it. Do not uncover the nakedness of your mother, step-mother, sister, half-sister, aunt on either side, daughter in law, granddaughter, an animal, another man and the list continues.

We might roll our eyes and point out that those verses are in the old covenant. The reality is the principle is also repeated in the New Testament. In other words the call for momogamy which is to be married to and faithful to one person of the opposite gender is very much a common and strong theme in the gospels and the epistles.

THERE IS AN ONGOING CALL TO EXCLUSIVE INTIMACY.

Jesus calls us to remember that in the beginning they were made man and woman and the two shall become one flesh;

4 "Haven't you read," he replied, "that at the beginning the Creator 'made them male and female,' 5 and said, 'For this reason a man will leave his father and mother and be united to his wife, and the two will become one flesh'? **6 So they are no longer two, but one flesh.**

Therefore what God has joined together, let no one separate." Matt 19:4-6

The one flesh idea is very powerful and represents a life long unity of love and commitment that is not to be shared as there is a special exclusivity. In the New Testament the emphasis is not so much on rules per se yet fences of protection are still very clear. Exclusivity in marriage with mind and body is very plain, but now in the inner power from the Spirit of Christ to become like Christ not from our own broken capacities. How then do we live as holy pure people?

Rules and the Law cannot be the empowering force as they cannot "subdue" our passions and desires as Paul clearly lays out in Colossians 2;

20If you have died with Christ to the spiritual forces of the world, why, as though you still belonged to the world, do you submit to its regulations: 21"Do not handle, do not taste, do not touch!"? 22These will all perish with use, because they are based on human commands and teachings. 23Such restrictions indeed have an appearance of wisdom, with their self-prescribed worship, their false humility, and their harsh treatment of the body; but they are of no value against the indulgence of the flesh.

It is common and correct to contrast the Old Testament with the New Testament but what do we really mean? What really is the difference? Is it the change from law and works to grace and faith? Yes, it most certainly is, though grace and faith are throughout the whole of the Old Testament as well. The most vivid contrast in the New Testament is emphatically pictured as being between the LAW and the SPIRIT. This is more important than we can imagine.

Let's examine the key differences between the Law and the Spirit;

- The law reveals sin

- The law condemns and kills
- The law enhances sin
- The law points to the command…to do…to work…

- The Spirit is power
- The Spirit is freedom
- The Spirit means death to our own efforts by faith
- The Spirit is surrender to all who God is and says
- The Spirit depends on faith
- The Spirit gives life

> **BY THE WAY….ON A BIG SCALE…JUST WHAT IS LAW?**
>
> This means any **laws** or **ways** or **principles** or **strategies** or **sacrifices** made or **wise proverbs** from worldly people or even **accountability** in and of itself or **reading more bible**…in and of itself… The Law of any kind… cannot deal with sin…full stop… we need the Spirit's power.

Back to the Three areas

1. That you should avoid sexual immorality…negative angle
2. That you should control your own body…positive angle
3. That you should not do wrong to a brother or sister…negative angle

Looking at these 3 areas in the positive we could re-state them as follows;

1. Be sexually intimate only with your spouse. 1 Corinthians 7 says to not defraud each other but to regularly come together.

2. Be filled with the Spirit as the Spirit enables us to exercise self control and in so doing we enhance the world of all those around about us. The truth is a person lacking self control is not a safe person.
3. In potentially vulnerable situations choose a way out so that both parties are protected. Do not wait for the other person to cooperate to do this as they may be too enmeshed to desire being free.

We must remember though that the Word of God chooses to use the **"non-positive"** means at times to make clear we fully appreciate what is out of bounds, what is damaging and what is an overflowing of the banks of the natural course of a river. I'll use an example to show why this "non-positive" approach is needed.

Marriage example

We can be told 100 times **to respect our wives…** this is in the positive form… but sometimes we need to be told the specifics from the negative angle as to how to do that.

It means **to not put her down ;**

> In public
> in private
> in front of the kids
> in front of yours or her parents!

It especially means **to not make jokes about her in any way;**

> her body
> her personality
> her capacities
> her lack in certain areas.

So… from the appropriate negative perspective;

1. avoid,
2. don't lose control
3. dont take advantage!

1. **Avoid sexual immorality…Greek= porneia**…anything that excites us sexually or gratifies our sexual desires outside of marriage.

Some of the best advice I have ever heard here is that to put out a fire a bigger fire must be burning! We must cultivate a fire for Christ by developing our prayer life and being honest about our struggles with God no matter how deep and dark and unacceptable they may appear to be as he knows anyway. Cry and groan if you have to but most all be honest. Have faith in his power to bring freedom and change into this area. Allow his love to fill you, to heal you, to refresh you. God has created us to be intimate with him and without this intimacy we will search for it elsewhere. Knowing truth in our heads won't quell the fires of lust. It is only when we have a passion for Christ demonstrated by constant prayer that we will see change.

"Quell"means to subdue, silence or suppress…is this the right word? Perhaps… "Overwhelm"with the holy fire of the presence of God might be an even better way to say it. If we are truly to give up something that grips us we must convinced that what we reach out to grab ahold of will be better otherwise why would we give it up?

2. **Control your own body…Don't lose control**

Literally this verse says "…to possess your own vessel."
A few bible translators have taken this to mean "be committed to your own wife and no-one else." This is of course the right thing to do

but is it what this verse is saying in particular? Generally the evidence (stronger support) leans toward saying that the vessel is our own body which we must take charge of. We must surrender our own bodies as living sacrifices daily and not demand our rights over our own bodies.

It is another way of saying Romans 12:1,2.

12 Therefore, I urge you, brothers and sisters, in view of God's mercy, **to offer your bodies** as a living sacrifice, holy and pleasing to God—this is your true and proper worship. **2** Do not conform to the pattern of this world, but be transformed by the renewing of your mind. Then you will be able to test and approve what God's will is—his good, pleasing and perfect will. NIV

Two seemingly opposite principles are inherent in this command;

2.1 Own your own body

Listen to what your body is saying but don't surrender ownership. The popular idea that the body must be listened to at all times has an element of truth and a whole lot of error! We do need healthy boundaries or we will be taken advantage of. Medically we need to "listen to" what our bodies are saying and not push ourselves beyond what we know we can cope with. This makes good physical sense though top athletes will emphatically state unless you "push yourself" at times you will never get stronger. We need to recognise when illness or disease is gripping our bodies and respond accordingly. We cannot do the same activities after an accident as time is needed to heal and rehabilitate. The word for the sinful nature though is the flesh and that is for a good reason. The sinful nature especially uses the body to operate through and in. It takes a "holy design element" and uses it for unholy purposes. The idea then is to take responsibility for your own choices and don't follow what your body is driving you to do. When tempted Christ will provide a way of escape as Paul so eloquently describes;

13No temptation has seized you except what is common to man. And God is faithful; He will not let you be tempted beyond what you can bear. But when you are tempted, He will also provide an escape, so that you can stand up under it.[55]

That is a a great promise, we can look around for the way of escape as God's word says there will always be one!

2.2 Relinquish ownership of your body to Christ….

Allowing Christ full control of your body is not at all a popular idea but much needed for spiritual maturity. It is so important we surrender our bodies to Christ as living sacrifices every day. This does not mean we have no boundaries so let me explain.

Physiotherapy example

Physiotherapists in their wisdom and experience also can push us beyond what our bodies can seem to cope with! Anyone who has had a serious injury and had extensive rehabilitation will know first hand what this means. We actually need to listen to them in those situations and not give in to our bodies which will be screaming out against the scar tissue being broken through to allow greater movement and flexibility.

How much more wise and experienced and sovereign and loving is Jesus Christ? Remember all those **"How much more"** statements that Jesus gave when comparing an earthly example to the work of his heavenly Father? Just as an earthly Father would not give a scorpion when a child asked for an egg (Luke 11:12) **"how much more…"** will our heavenly Father give the Holy Spirit (Luke 11:13) and good gifts (Matthew 7:11) to his children. We must become living sacrifices just like Isaac though in a spiritual sense. The "right" to use our body in whatever way

---

[55] 1 Corinthians 10:13

we please is gone. It is now up to Christ and he will always protect and guard and do what is right. How contrary this is to the loud clamour of "our body, our rights" In the world. An even sadder truth is that some of that protest is actually taking away the rights of the unborn little body being carried within who is actually a separate person to the mother and who has no voice of their own.

3. **Do not take advantage of a brother or sister**

We do have to ask the question about what we might be doing that either cultivates a hunger for sexual expression by knowingly or otherwise enticing others or even seducing them.

Perhaps we have unconsciously or otherwise realised that they have gone through some difficult times so are more inclined to cross boundaries in order to feel good about themselves. Our fleshly side can begin to operate and strategise and get to work.

Loneliness is a powerful force and unless we are filled up with the Spirit of God then truth alone will not be enough for our hearts. There are plenty of "doctrine filled people" whose lives are in a mess! I don't just mean heretics and cult leaders either.

Perhaps we might want to still be considered young, spritely and attractive so by flirting even a little, by playing with fire, we attempt to raise our flagging self esteem. This modus operandi is a subtle thing and not always easily recognisable. We need to become "sober and alert" and people of the light in order to quickly recognise such activity. When we feed our own lusts we can easily draw another into the feeding frenzy and lead them into sin. We drag others down in whatever type of sin we commit but sexual sin does extreme damage as it ends up with boundaries crossed, hearts broken and lives in disarray. It is a very core method of the evil one to "wreak great havoc." Many say that it felt so right or that we were both willing parties yet in reality one had to lead and one had to be susceptible and open to being led.

- Damage is done in ways we cannot even imagine.
- We can be so willingly blind at the time.
- The ripple effect is huge though we struggle to deny it.
- What it promises it never delivers.

It is for the sake of his name that we walk in righteousness.[56] He will empower us by faith as we choose to obey in order to please him.

The call is to exclusive intimacy with Christ. For some like Paul that is enough. Yet for those who are married it is expressed in an exclusive intimacy with our spouse. To the single person desiring marriage in the future the surrender is expressed in the wait. If we have "sexual issues" in our marriage we must turn to Christ for love and not cast our gaze elsewhere. Holiness is powerful and life changing and enables us to "see the Lord."[57] Let us never forget the God of grace who forgives our every sin yet let us also not forget it is the perfect will of God that we be sanctified.

For the Church to be healthy it is called to be an exclusive lover to Christ. This is reflected in the way we live as sexual beings in the physical realm. We are not to commit sexual immorality, we are not to lose control of our own bodies and we are not to take advantage of one another.

---

[56] Psalm 23:3
[57] Hebrews 12:14

9
The Second Coming Triplet

The Church is complete at the last trumpet blast
REVEALED, RESURRECTED, REUNITED

1 Thessalonians 4:13-18

Believers Who Have Died

13 Brothers and sisters, we do not want you to be uninformed about those who sleep in death, so that you do not grieve like the rest of mankind, who have no hope. **14** For we believe that Jesus died and rose again, and so we believe that God will bring with Jesus those who have fallen asleep in him. **15** According to the Lord's word, we tell you that we who are still alive, who are left until the coming of the Lord, will certainly not precede those who have fallen asleep. **16** For the Lord himself will come down from heaven, with a loud command, with the voice of the archangel and with the trumpet call of God, and the dead in Christ will rise first. **17** After that, we who are still alive and are left will be caught up together with them in the clouds to meet the Lord in the air. And so we will be with the Lord forever. **18** Therefore encourage one another with these words.

Context

What is the concern here?

Remember that Paul had taught over 3 sabbaths so had been there for approximately 15 days. The teaching he had given was that Jesus was coming back again and we must be watching as no-one knows the hour nor the day. Now time had gone on and some saved people had died since the church was formed. They clearly had loved the Lord and led godly lives but what was to come of them as they died before Jesus came back?

Had those older folk or sick kids missed out because they departed before Jesus returned? Was the situation hopeless for them? If it was a matter of "bad timing" then it seems just so unfair. Paul chooses to reply by dealing with both the essential nature of born again human beings and life after death in the interim period as well as touching on aspects of Jesus return and finally life eternal. This is a pastoral and compassionate response to a real worry. He is not just "clearing up bad doctrine" but wrapping his arms around them and giving great comfort in his tender response. He is certainly not rebuking them for getting it so wrong as his heart is always for the person before their belief system. When the situation arises Paul is totally prepared to rebuke arrogant and stubborn people who cause division in the body but that is an altogether different matter.

They did not know the full picture as they were 'uninformed.'
"We do not want you to be ignorant"...
Here we have yet again a **"biblical non-positive." General positives** sometimes fail to help us to see what we need to "stop" doing. Hence there is the need to outline the wrong and the evil and the ugly, to really spell it out at times. This time it is to move them from one place to the next from ignorance to knowledge, from sadness to hope. To translate

with a "positive" such as "we want you to know" [58] actually dilutes the strength of this verse. Paul through the Spirit emphatically states "…we **do not want** you to be **ignorant**."

It is not uncaring to be honest about a position someone holds and help them move from ignorance to truth, from unbelief to faith. Despite the powerful influence of our "feelings centred contemporary culture" the reality is many times the truth can and will eventually make all the difference. It is not just kind words or a hug or a listening ear or a pathway through the grief as necessary and preliminary as those things frequently are.

The truth is ultimately the pathway to healing as the truth is Christ himself. He is not separate from his words. It is the tension between hearing what the other person has to say and when appropriate sharing the truth from above into a situation that ultimately needs the power of God.

Paul is about to move into saying "we believe." In other words our faith in this truth will bring real hope and enable you to see into something that is incredibly beautiful. You will be able to move from hopeless grief like the world experiences through to a **"faith filled fullness"** because you now know God's plan which cannot be altered, thwarted, debated or dismissed. The divine blueprint is unfolding every day without any human interference as he is truly sovereign. Human grief for unbelievers, for those who don't have hope, is a shattering experience. Many times I have seen people at funerals quake, wail and weep deeply out of a loss that to them is forever permanent. It is a sad and heartbreaking thing to watch and be a part of.

Death is described as the last enemy as only in Christ is it taken away. Without the victory of Christ **"over death from among the dead"**

---

[58] NLT And now, dear brothers and sisters, we want you to know what will happen to the believers who have died so you will not grieve like people who have no hope.

we have a hopeless picture.[59] Death is indeed a grim reaper that has the last laugh and there is no return. We will for a time just become compost for the soil as the Word of God graphically describes this return to the earth from which we came. We will not become a star, a butterfly or an angel which contemporary celebrants use as their soft and gentle worldly healing balm and throw such ideas like pixie dust over the bereaved.

Paul describes those who "have fallen asleep in death" and it is quite literally exactly that in the Greek. It is clearly not just for a few hours or just in a coma though. It is an expression intended to enable us to see the non-permanent nature of death. It speaks of getting ready for a change, of a metamorphosis about to occur in the future.

Jesus also spoke of those who had died as having fallen asleep. Mark describes the occasion when the 12 year old daughter of Jairus the Synagogue "head honcho" became very ill and before Jesus arrived she actually passed away. Here is the story;

> 38When they arrived at the house of the synagogue leader, Jesus saw the commotion and the people weeping and wailing loudly. 39He went inside and asked, "Why all this commotion and weeping? The child is not dead, but asleep." 40And they laughed at Him. After He had put them all outside, He took the child's father and mother and His own companions, and went in to see the child. 41Taking her by the hand, Jesus said, "Talitha koum!" which means, "Little girl, I say to you, get up!" 42Immediately the girl got up and began to walk around. She was twelve years old, and at once they were utterly astounded. 43Then Jesus gave strict orders that no one should know about this, and He told them to give her something to eat.[60]

---

[59] (Romans 6:9 quite literally in the Greek has the sense of being risen from among all those who are dead.)

[60] Mark 5:38-43. BSB

Jesus said to her *"Talitha koum"* which is Aramaic for **"little girl get up."** Lazarus when dead was also described as having fallen asleep. Jesus has the power to raise the dead and to one who can see the beginning from the end anyone who dies and is saved has actually **"fallen asleep in Jesus."** Paul in this passage is describing a time when it will not just be individuals who come back to life with their original mortal bodies once again to die. This time is a brand new paradigm where at Christ's return "they will be raised to immortality." Paul elaborates further on this when he writes to the Corinthians;

52 in an instant, in the twinkling of an eye, at the last trumpet. For the trumpet will sound, the dead will be raised imperishable, and we will be changed. **53 For the perishable must be clothed with the imperishable, and the mortal with immortality.** [61]

Paul in our original passage is about to describe a reunion that is beyond description. It will be a drawing together in "the sky" of all believers who have ever lived. A gathering of the family, of transformed brothers and sisters, on a level of perfection that is like nothing we can even imagine. Let's quickly hear what John has to say because it's too good to miss!

3 See what great love the Father has lavished on us, that we should be called children of God! And that is what we are! The reason the world does not know us is that it did not know him. **2 Dear friends, now we are children of God, and what we will be has not yet been made known. But we know that when Christ appears, we shall be like him, for we shall see him as he is. 3** All who have this hope in him purify themselves, just as he is pure. [62]

---

[61] 1Corinthians 15:51-53 BSB
[62] 1 John 3:1-3

John says we are first of all children of God which declares we have an unencumbered entrance into the family of heaven where love will be further lavished upon us. We don't even realise how magnificent our future will be as it's just too great to comprehend. John enthusiastically continues by saying that when we see him in the air we shall be like him. This is our hope, this is what enables us to stay pure, this waiting for his return and all it entails. This Greek word for "appearing" here in 1 John 3:2 is φανερόω pronounced "phaneroo." This word means to make plain, to be clearly visible, to be manifested, to be seen by all. This meaning is important as we move through this passage. Here in 1 Thessalonians 4 we get some other details about his appearing. The Greek word in 1 Thessalonians is παρουσία pronounced "Parousia" which means the coming or arrival or personal presence of a dignitary, often meaning a royal arrival. **Putting the two ideas together, as I believe we have license to do, we get a very visible royal arrival on a grand scale!** This very visible arrival on a global scale is described by Jesus when he talks of future events with his disciples;

26 "So if anyone tells you, 'There he is, out in the wilderness,' do not go out; or, 'Here he is, in the inner rooms,' do not believe it. **27 For as lightning that comes from the east is visible** even in the west, so will be the coming of the Son of Man.[63]

We believe Jesus himself has paved the way and is the basis for this hope. He died but then overcame death as it could not hold him down. Because he did what could not be done, which was previously impossible, he now has the authority, power and right to grant us the same which is life after death, victory over the grave. Such a tone of conquest is very evident as we read Paul's crescendo in his teaching on the resurrection to the Corinthians;

---

[63] Matthew 24:26-27

...54When the perishable has been clothed with the imperishable and the mortal with immortality, then the saying that is written will come to pass: "**Death has been swallowed up in victory.**" 55"Where, O Death, is your victory? Where, O Death, is your sting?"[64]

All of this leads us to our teaching triplet. It builds to a grouping of ideas describing the completion of Christ's saving work for all believers at his return.

The Future Hope Triplet

The eternal undying spirits of those who have died will accompany Jesus when he returns
    The bodies of these believers will be transformed when their perfect spirits merge with their new body
    Living believers will be transformed also and join this host from heaven and be with the Lord forever

1. Perfect spirits of promoted believers return with Jesus

REVEALED

14 For we believe that Jesus died and rose again, and so we believe that God will bring with Jesus those who have fallen asleep in him.

Did you hear the story of the sonata being played backwards as the gravedigger in Vienna went off to work each day?.... it was Beethoven decomposing. I told that old joke during a sermon just recently and it still gets a modest laugh or maybe a groan? If you dig up a grave six months later you will find a rotten body whether they were believers or unbelievers. They rot the same, they decompose the same, they "push up daisies" the same. Our spirits fly to "our home in heaven" the

---

[64]   1 Cor 15:54-55

moment we die and the body is left behind. We can rightly call heaven **"the presence of God where there is no imperfection"** for those who are already in a frenzy for someone to have the gall to describe heaven in geographical terms! Paul was a tentmaker so it wasn't a big jump for him to compare our frail bodies to the tents he made to earn his living as he describes to the Corinthians;

1**Now we know that if the earthly tent** we live in is dismantled, we have a building from God, an eternal house in heaven, not built by human hands. 2**For in this tent we groan**, longing to be clothed with our heavenly dwelling, 3because when we are clothed, we will not be found naked. 4**So while we are in this tent**, we groan under our burdens, because we do not wish to be unclothed but clothed, so that our mortality may be swallowed up by life. 5And God has prepared us for this very purpose and has given us the Spirit as a pledge of what is to come.65

Verse 6 in this same passage says;

"We are confident, then, and would prefer to be away from the body and **at home with the Lord.**"

The Greek word for "at home" is endemeo…ἐνδημέω. The idea as stated in Strong's concordance is "to properly, be present (at home), as amongst one's own type of (kindred, related) people."**At home** then means to be "where I truly belong" which in this case means with the Lord and my own perfect saved and redeemed kin!

We still use the old English phrase "With kith and kin" which literally means "my native home country **and** my relatives." In other words the surroundings of our loved and familiar environment as well as our own people who are close to our heart. Indigenous people in Australia will tend to use the expression "my peoples' country." You will hear them

---

65   2 Cor 5:1-5.

talk of "my mother's country" or something similar. It is our spirit that goes to be with the Lord when we die. We leave our old tent behind, this groaning tent ("tell me about it!" says anyone over a certain vintage!) that is about to be dismantled. Our mortality we believe by faith is about to be swallowed up in life. Our spirits are eternal as they live forever but a new incorruptible body is needed! There is an alternative viewpoint about the permanence of the human spirit however called the doctrine of annihilation.

> **The doctrine of annihilation** *while not being universally agreed upon has as its central tenet the idea that immediately after death and judgement the spirits of unbelievers are extinguished and cease to exist. The debate hinges to some extent on the true meaning of words such as "perish" and "destroyed." Just think of John 3:16 where if we "believe in him" we will not "perish." Perish would then come to mean "the complete annihilation of the human spirit." I believe that this teaching probably does not do justice to the incredible nature of the human spirit made in the image of God. Our human reasoning clamours for some leniency in the "eternal punishment" mandate yet Scripture as far as I can see seems to indicate otherwise. The divinely created human spirit is eternally of value and the annihilation of such seems to contradict and downplay its immense value. Having just entered briefly into the debate let me say that unless we are gripped deeply about the horrific idea of anyone going to hell we shouldn't really be even having this discussion! God does not force us to spend eternity with him. The reality is if we don't want to be with him forever he is not going to make us do so. There is only one other option though and it is very frightening in its nature and duration. The creation of the unbiblical idea of* **purgatory** *is different again as it*

seeks to bring everyone eventually into heaven after our allotted period of punishment. This seems to me to cut out both the sacrifice of Christ on our behalf and to force people into God's holy presence whether they wanted to be there or not! The duration of our time in purgatory is said to be able to be influenced by doing certain righteous acts on behalf of the person who has died effectively removing personal accountability. Does our modern and limited sense of justice have to have every 'fallen human box" ticked or can we allow God to reveal to us what is perfect and right? Is God the epitome of wisdom and truth and justice and love or is he a flawed deity that needs our help to pick up on those areas he hasn't worked through well enough? I believe his ways are higher than our ways and his thoughts higher than our thoughts and he is perfect in all of his ways. He will also never give up on loving his creation with a love that is described by Charles Wesley as "love divine, all love excelling."

2. Perfect spirits become one with brand new immortal bodies

RESURRECTED

The eternal spirits of saints that have gone on ahead of us, being already perfected in Christ finally become one with their new immortal bodies. Hebrews 12 tells us that even now we have not come to a physical mountain like Mt Sinai that could not be touched without fear of death but;

22Instead, you have come to Mount Zion, to the city of the living God, the heavenly Jerusalem. You have come to myriads of angels 23in joyful assembly, to the congregation of the firstborn, enrolled in heaven.

You have come to God the Judge of all, **to the spirits of the righteous made perfect,**

> Believers are made perfect the moment we die and dwell in Christ in his presence.

16 For the Lord himself will come down from heaven, with a loud command, with the voice of the archangel and with the trumpet call of God, **and the dead in Christ will rise first.**

Jesus is described as being at the right hand side of the Father. His is the name above every name. He is even now ruling from heaven. He is truly the King of Kings. Jesus is the Lord! He is the supreme ruler, Almighty God, through whom all things are created.

HE WILL COME DOWN FROM HEAVEN…!

This is pictured graphically in Revelation 19 which explores this truth in a more comprehensive way. If Revelation is considered to be a series of cycles and not linear history the "end" is described a number of times in this apocalyptic vision. We see it once again described in Revelation 19 and again with different details in Revelation 20. This is how I tend to interpret this magnificent book of spiritual symbolism that reveals historical realities in a series of cycles in incredibly graphic form. A loud command, the voice of the arch angel and the trumpet call of God. This is such a contrast to the first Christmas, the first coming. Compare here the two comings;

- in humility…in glory…
- in obscurity…in revelation of his Lordship…
- in the flesh…in the Spirit …
- In weakness…in power…
- in service…in majesty.

A loud command

The Lion of Judah has the voice of authority unlike any other being.

His voice is described elsewhere as being like the sound of rushing waters;

14The hair of His head was white like wool, as white as snow, and His eyes were like a blazing fire. 15 His feet were like polished bronze refined in a furnace, and His voice was like the roar of many waters. Revelation 1:14-15

1Then the man brought me back to the gate that faces east, 2and I saw the glory of the God of Israel coming from the east. His voice was like the roar of many waters, and the earth shone with His glory. Ezekiel 43:1-2

There is no voice like the sound of Almighty God. No-one will dare challenge such authority, glory and majesty at his appearing. All leaders will freeze in their tracks and fall down. All philosophers and atheists will be overcome by a shout that drowns out their minuscule bleating. All oppressed people will rise up at the sound of the deliverer, at such a voice of justice. The Good Shepherd who leads out his sheep one by one with such a gentle voice now thunders as his identity as the commander of the hosts of heaven and of all the universe is dramatically revealed. The Lion of Judah will roar with an intensity that penetrates our very bones. There will be no continuation of what we have known as all will change in an instant. When Elohim created the world it is said he just spoke and all the universe came into being. We cannot imagine such creative wonder. Yet this time there will be a shout! It will be like nothing else we have ever heard before. All rebellion will cease at that moment as the Lord will truly thunder from heaven!

The voice of the Arch-angel

The chief angel is Michael. The most powerful celestial created being. He is possessed with unimaginable might and authority yet totally subject to the king, the Ancient of days. Jehovah's Witnesses believe that Michael is a name given to Jesus before and after his time on earth. [66]In other words Jesus to them is a created being. This is in order to fit into their "reason based and logical religious framework" that cannot cope with revealed spiritual realities such as the Godhead, the three in one, the trinity. There is no doubt that Michael does the bidding of Christ yet he is not the same. He is under the authority of Jesus Christ, the Lord of all.

The trumpet call of God

The "trumpet" in the Bible was generally the long horn of a Ram. Growing up on a farm in the northern wheatbelt of WA with Merino sheep I learnt to keep out of the way of the horns of any ram no matter what size they were! Having now seen an example of the rams' horns on Israeli sheep proudly owned by a contemporary Messianic Jew called David who spent some time in Alice Springs with his wife Deborah I must admit they seem even more formidable and clearly could produce a blast that was heard for considerable distance. The blast of the Ram's horn known by the Jews as the shofar in Scripture is very significant. It was used in the following instances;

- Anointing of a King
- Announcing the Sabbath and the new Moon
- A call to war
- A call for moral reform
- A blast from heaven
- Alikened to the holy prophetic cry

---

[66] jw.org bible teachings "Who is the Archangel Michael ?"

Paul describes this same last trumpet in 1 Corinthians 15;

51 Behold! I tell you a mystery. We shall not all sleep, but we shall all be changed, **52** in a moment, in the twinkling of an eye, **at the last trumpet. For the trumpet will sound,** and the dead will be raised imperishable, and we shall be changed.

This blast signifies a passing from one era to the next. It announces the termination of our time based confinement to an altogether new timeless unrestricted eternity. The bodies of the dead in Christ, no matter how separated each molecule may be from each other, are powerfully rejoined and made into a new spiritual body like the body of Jesus Christ. I remember as a child in the 1970's the cartoon gospel tracts made by Chick publications that graphically showed each tiny part of a body no matter what had happened to the person all coming back together to form the new resurrected body! It was quite gripping and the image still remains with me. I have learnt over the years that the word of God can be dramatically portrayed through art and therefore preaching should not just be limited to words alone. This is especially so in certain cultures that are extremely visual where the impact of a Holy Spirit inspired picture can be powerful. A number of churches in Alice Springs used a 16 picture banner designed by indigenous and non-indigenous artists called "God's Dreaming"[67] to illustrate the most significant aspects of the bible story and had it mounted on a wall in the church. We at Alice Baptist began a process of preaching through "a picture a month" and it was still happening when I shifted back to Perth. Yuendumu Baptist church out in the Tanami had done this much earlier with a unique set of designs made by the Warlpiri people that grab your attention the moment you enter the Yuendumu Baptist chapel.

This new body is joined with the spirits of those made perfect to form the new whole person who will dwell forever with Christ. This

---

[67] http://www.godsdreaming.org/

is a mystery that was becoming much clearer. This resurrection of the body is a transformation by the Spirit into a spiritual body designed for eternity with the eternal human spirit resident within.

3. All believers caught up together in the air
REUNITED

Living believers will also be transformed and join this host from heaven and be with the Lord forever. We will be receiving our new bodies and having our spirits perfected on the way, in the twinkling of an eye. We will be lifted out of an earth that is about to be judged and consumed. Peter goes to great lengths to describe this final reality;

3 Above all, you must understand that in the last days scoffers will come, scoffing and following their own evil desires. **4** They will say, "Where is this 'coming' he promised? Ever since our ancestors died, everything goes on as it has since the beginning of creation." **5** But they deliberately forget that long ago by God's word the heavens came into being and the earth was formed out of water and by water. **6** By these waters also the world of that time was deluged and destroyed. **7 By the same word the present heavens and earth are reserved for fire, being kept for the day of judgment and destruction of the ungodly.** [68]

The great gathering in the sky or great reunion in the air is the family of the Father from all periods of time, saved by the blood of his son, finally together by the Spirit to start the journey of eternity where love reigns and righteousness dwells. It is also the bridegroom coming for his bride, for the one he loves and is committed to with a holy exclusivity. No wonder Paul and Peter and John say that if we have this hope we will purify ourselves as he is pure. We are woo-ed in order to ready and prepare ourselves for the wedding, for the marriage, for the eternal union

---

[68] 2 Peter 3:3-7

with the Son. Eye has not seen nor ear heard nor mind conceived what God has prepared in advance for those who love him. Here are the words of an old hymn by Edgar M Pace that capture the essence of these truths.

That Glad Reunion Day

Verse 1
There will be a happy meeting in heaven I know,
When we see the many loved ones we've known here below;
Gather on the blessed hilltops with hearts all aglow,
That will be a glad reunion day.

Chorus
Glad (That will be a happy day) day, Yes, a wonderful day,
Glad (That will be a happy day) day, Yes, a glorious day,
There with all the holy angels and loved ones to stay,
That will be a glad reunion day.

Verse 2
There within the holy city we'll sing and rejoice,
Praising Christ the blessed Savior with heart and with voice;
Tell Him how we came to love Him and make Him our choice,
That will be a glad reunion day.

Verse 3
When we live a million years in that wonderful place,
Basking in the love of Jesus, beholding His face,
It will seem but just a moment of praising His grace,
That will be a glad reunion day.

The Church will be complete at the return of Christ. There will be a mighty revelation of the Son of God and the spirits of those made perfect will accompany him in a glorious entrance from heaven to earth. There will be a powerful raising from the dead of past believers bodies. These new resurrected bodies like Christ's own body will then be joined with their eternal perfect spirits. This will all result in an amazing reunion of all believers in the family of God from every tribe and tongue and era.

10

The day of the Lord Triplet

The church is a warning beacon to the world
NO WARNING: LIKE A THIEF IN THE NIGHT
NO WORRIES: DURING A TIME OF SECURITY
NO ESCAPE: IMPOSSIBLE TO RUN FROM.

---

1 Thessalonians 5:1-3

5 Now, brothers and sisters, about times and dates we do not need to write to you, 2 for you know very well that **the day of the Lord** will come like a thief in the night. 3 While people are saying, "Peace and safety," destruction will come on them suddenly, as labor pains on a pregnant woman, and they will not escape.

What is the true purpose of preaching?

It is to unveil, unfold, and uncover the will of God in the word of God for the glory of God to the people of God and finally to the whole world. It is to declare everything that is revealed to us about the mystery who is Christ and what he has done to gain for himself a holy people.

Using a biblical description regarding the breathed out word of God these words by Paul also show us the purpose of preaching;

All Scripture is God-breathed and is useful for teaching, rebuking, correcting and training in righteousness. 2 Tim 3:16

In preaching we cannot be piecemeal or selective, we must deal with the whole counsel of God.

- To not just preach what is popular... in the church.
- To not just echo the world ... the latest fad.
- To not preach what is expected....but to enable God's people to see the reason for each theme and idea
- To not just make people feel safe....but to grow valiant disciples of Jesus Christ

The church has been accused of answering the questions nobody is asking. That probably sounds like a wise and considered reproof to the church and in some quarters it probably is. There is another angle to this "reproof" that must be carefully considered. Our purpose in both evangelism and preaching is to point people to the questions that lie deep within but often are as of yet unexpressed. We are called to dig deep to reveal the questions that all people have whether they know it or not. In essence we are mandated to lead people to places they may not naturally want to go but desperately need to do so. We do this in order to reveal the light of the gospel in the face of Christ who is the answer to all our questions.

The church can't keep on adjusting to the feedback the world gives us as to how to be better. All too frequently a well intentioned business person or educator in the church gives "good advice" to the preacher or leadership team as to what the latest research is saying concerning structure, pedagogy or marketing. Some of these things do have a place yet more often than not they depend on worldly wisdom and are driven by commercial approaches. Our call is to know our God, to go deeper into his Word, discover the new wineskins that hold the new wine of the new covenant and obey what we have been given in prayer and fasting by the power of the Spirit. We have to model to the world a powerful church whether they give us a good score or not!

The power of reading whole bible books

A common contemporary church trend is to focus purely on the positives. After all isn't the gospel the good news? Sometimes there is an inexplicable anger when the whole truth is preached and I mean even in bible believing churches. We must allow the following principles to guide us and not keep people in a matrix of upbeat reality avoiding superficiality;

- The light shines brightest in the deepest darkness
- The thirst for Hope is greater when life is truly hopeless
- A life rope is clung to when we know we are drowning

Movement within a letter covers many diverse themes

Here in 1 Thessalonians the themes move from deep faith to being like a father to sexual purity to the second coming as it is not a whole treatise on one particular theme. The gospels are the same as they do appear at times to jump from one thought to the next. There is a continuity though that after soaking in the word becomes clearer. There is a definite connectedness yet usually only from one angle or theme at a time. **The Word of God deals with the same topics from other perspectives in other gospels and other letters as this is God's deliberate plan in his seamless word.** In many ways this lets us see the pedagogical mastery of the teacher of teachers. We learn best it would appear when we deal with one subject a little at a time and then slowly digest it and absorb it into our spiritual tissues enabling this new food to give us the life we need. It also reveals to us we mustn't build a whole doctrine from just one book, especially a symbolic book.

Parallel with gym training

We can just focus on one part of the body or form of exercise and while it will have real benefit and even some overflow into other parts of our body we can nevertheless become unbalanced. We need to be willing therefore to do the uncomfortable types of routines to become stronger overall. We just might need that extra exercise routine one day as it rounds us out and also prevents injury down the track. There is benefit to all areas when we work on an additional area as everything is connected in our body. It is always time to develop muscles we didn't know we had in both the physical and spiritual realms! It is an invitation to do extra training in a crucial area without which we would be weaker overall. A good example is doing core muscle work as a runner. We end up with lots of issues in the legs when we neglect the core muscle groups in the abdominal area. It may seem unrelated but it ends up having a significant impact.

The next triplet is very much a "neglected muscle group" in many churches today yet we neglect it at our peril. In a few churches it is the only muscle group that is trained and becomes swollen and distorted which is another problem altogether.

The Day of the Lord

Paul spoke about "the day of the Lord" when he was in Thessalonica.

The day of the Lord was part of his edification of the believers and a warning to unbelievers. It was therefore part and parcel of his ecclesiology and his evangelism. To share the message and life of Christ in the cross, the resurrection, and the promise of eternal life without the reality of the day of the Lord would be incomplete in the mind of the Apostle who is carried along by the Spirit as he dictates this letter to his scribe.

- Why think about the next life if no disaster is imminent?
- Why cry out for help if the end isn't nigh?
- Why ask for forgiveness when you've not done anything wrong?

Inseparable from the second coming?

Paul seems to speak of the church being caught up in the clouds, the second coming of Jesus Christ and the destruction of the world as being all part of the single day of the Lord. Others see a considerable gap between the two or even three ideas. Whether you see no gap at all, a five to six month gap, a three and half to seven year gap or a 1000 year gap the reality is the same as to the details of the judgement aspect of the day of the Lord and that is what I will focus on.

Old Testament prophets often spoke of the day of the Lord. Sometimes it referred to a day of immediate judgement in their time and day but often it simultaneously referred to a big final day (time) of judgement over the whole earth. It is a common theme in nearly all the prophetic literature.

Sandwich board guys... repent the end is nigh...

How have we responded as a church to images of bearded sandwich board and poster wielding radicals calling us to repent for the end is nigh? Have we looked with horror as we recoil in the fear that others might think that somehow we believe the same thing? In our heart of hearts are they considered to just be caricatures and not to be seen as part of the body of Christ? Have we been hoodwinked into rejecting what in some instances is actually the will of God? Have we joined the world and run away from such mocking because we are afraid to be tainted with it? Peter tells us the world mocks anything about the second coming. When they do just how do we respond? Do we shy away from whatever is being mocked? Do we distance ourselves from anything the world says they think is ridiculous or funny or wrong? Whole churches are now designed to make sure we never get mocked by the world yet there is something seriously wrong with that approach. They enthusiastically and liberally gush with such acceptable terms like relevance, community and approachability. The Apostles and early Church would wonder what was going on. It is often the lack of "results" and "true power" that leads to such an approach though. The bible says it is time for serious surrender to the Spirit and Word instead of adopting worldly approaches to being the people of God.

We met a couple in Alice Springs who were dragging a cross around Australia and NZ. I wasn't too sure of their motives initially but after being in a combined Churches prayer meeting led by Ben and Rebecca Matson from "the church for all people" I realised how full of the Spirit this itinerant couple was and just how effective their ministry was. They have talked to hundreds of people about Christ and continue to do the will of God through their unique ministry. God clearly calls us all to do different things for him and in his name. Let's not box each other but celebrate the unique ways we all reach the world for Christ. Now that is true diversity of a kind that our Father in heaven delights in. Every single one of these triplets in this series teaches us a powerful truth about the nature of being the church. What triplet is connected to the day of the Lord?

1. The Day of the lord will come like a thief in the night

A thief doesn't leave a note or send a quick text to say when he's dropping in! A thief is more likely to come when we are asleep or away from the house as "darkness is their hour."

"I do not need to write to you about times and dates...."

So many people have sought to work out the date of the Lord's return and many other matters related to the final days. They have used mathematical methods and numerology[69] and all sorts of other means. Yet so many have been proved embarrassingly wrong.

Listen to this quote from "Edmond life and leisure."[70]

Among the most prolific modern predictors of end times, **Harold Camping** *has publicly predicted the end of the world as many as 12 times based on his interpretations of biblical numerology. In 1992, he published a book, ominously titled 1994? which predicted the end of the world sometime around that year. Perhaps his most high-profile predication was for May 21, 2011, a date that he calculated to be exactly 7,000 years after the Biblical flood. When that date passed without incident, he declared his math to be off and pushed back the end of the world to October 21, 2011.*

The day of the Lord will be like a thief as there will be no warning given. It does not mean that the invader won't be seen as it is not uncommon for a thief to be caught in the act despite his desire to remain unseen.

One more example of false declarations of the coming King;

Beginning when she was 42 years old, **Joanna Southcott** *reported hearing voices that predicted future events, including the crop failures and famines of 1799 and 1800. She began publishing her own books and eventually developed a following of as many as 100,000 believers. In 1813, she announced that in the following year she would give birth to the second messiah, whose arrival would signal the last days of the Earth—despite being 64 years old and, as she told her doctors, a virgin. She died before a baby could be born.*[71]

The key point is there will be no apparent warning so we need to be ready now.

---

[69] Not the same as the symbolic use of numbers such as "7" representing perfection. This symbolic usage is actually a key way that the Word of God teaches us about the ways of God.

[70] A Weekly Oklahoma newspaper

[71] brittanica.com "10 Failed Doomsday predictions."

Just like in the days of Noah;

37 As it was in the days of Noah, so it will be at the coming of the Son of Man. **38** For in the days before the flood, people were eating and drinking, marrying and giving in marriage, up to the day Noah entered the ark; **39 and they knew nothing about what would happen until the flood came and took them all away.** That is how it will be at the coming of the Son of Man. [72]

Noah was a preacher of righteousness but only 8 people were saved. Only 8 people entered the ark and were rescued on the day of the flood which was clearly and unambiguously the day of the Lord's terrible judgement. The day of the Lord will come, it will come! We are called to live by faith in the promise of God who has made it clear that this is not just the talk of "wild-eyed, placard waving crazy people!" There are always the two dimensions of the day of the Lord and that is perhaps why there is a lot of confusion regarding its nature. There is the delightful lifesaving rescue and deliverance aspect and there is the terrifying judgment and destruction from which there is no escape.

We have to also acknowledge that there is a warning dimension if we are prepared to see it. As the pre-flood people watched Noah build the ark and wondered why he was doing it they were being warned of what was to come but chose to only mock instead.

The constant warning signals

The creator loves human beings more than all the animals, which means even the cutest little puppy! The cost of some of these designer pets, especially if it is a groodle, poodle or caboodle is amazing nowadays and so are their veterinarian costs! It seems somehow very wrong for millions of children to die around the world for lack of food or health

---

[72] Matthew 24:37-39

supplies while thousands of dollars are spent on a single pet. Having just said that the grief of losing a much loved dog, cat or horse or even a budgie is considerable and I do not mean to downplay this for the lonely and the childless especially.

All humans are made in the image of God and we are told that even angels in all their glory are not given as high a status. I wonder then if anyone in that "ark building time" who had believed Noah and repented would have been allowed on? Did they take the time to listen to what this holy man was saying and declaring by the building of such a craft over a 100 year period? If you think your pastor goes on a bit on Sunday morning just think what a long and powerful sermon Noah preached! There is a human preference to remain blind to an impending catastrophe and act as if everything will just go on as per normal. We want to believe that things will never really change. Too often we hear of people staying in the face of a roaring fire or a rapidly rising flood only to suddenly discover it is too late and they should have left hours or even days ago. This is what Peter addresses in 2 Peter 3 where he says the old earth was taken out by water and the current one will be taken out with fire. The rainbow is a promise to not flood the earth again with water yet it does not prevent the horrifying flood of fire that will consume this physical earth with an intensity that will be unrivalled. There is coming a day when time itself will tick its last tock ushering in a new era of perfection.

There is a clear warning going out daily.

Pause to think of the nature of God revealed in the sky and the heavens and in creation, in the rhythm of the seasons, in day and night, in beauty and stillness and especially in the birth of a new born baby.

Psalm 19

1 The heavens declare the glory of God, the skies proclaim the work of his hands.
2 Day after day they pour forth speech; night after night they reveal knowledge.
3 They have no speech, they use no words; no sound is heard from them.
4 Yet their voice goes out into all the earth, their words to the ends of the world.

- **There is warning** going out through the radio waves and the TV and the internet through evangelists and preachers. Yes, God even uses internet preachers no matter what we might think!
- **There is warning** going out through Gideons bibles left in hotel rooms and given out to students and nurses and tracts handed out down the street and even in Carols by Candlelight services !
- **There is warning** going out when our lives fall apart and we cry out to God for help knowing deep down that there is no-one else who can truly put Humpty together again.
- **There is warning** going out as missionaries risk their lives and the persecuted church hangs on despite suffering.

2. The Day of the lord will be in a time of security and peace

The scenario given is like when a fire begins in a house during a party or a car crashes through the bedroom wall while we are sleeping or reading a book. There will be a celebration of life without God as all is going swimmingly! We just don't need him anymore. Look how good it is to live without a divine dictator peering over the edge of heaven looking down to whack us whenever we do wrong. How good it is to be free from guilt and able to live our own lives with a sense of independence. What is guilt anyway, surely it is nothing more than just a societal construct designed by twisted people to control your life, to keep you from having fun and doing what we really want to do….such party poopers! Finally humanity has (yet again) come of age, it has grown up, it has thrown off the shackles of a divine being. Isaiah spoke of such a malaise among the people of Israel a long time ago....

8Go now, write it on a tablet in their presence and inscribe it on a scroll;
it will be for the days to come,
a witness forever and ever.
9These are rebellious people, deceitful children,
children unwilling to obey the LORD's instruction.
10They say to the seers,
"Stop seeing visions!"
and to the prophets,
"Do not prophesy to us the truth!
Speak to us pleasant words;
prophesy illusions.
11Get out of the way; turn off the road.
Rid us of the Holy One of Israel!"[73]

Into this milieu, right at the end of time will come **"The Day of the Lord!"** While people are saying peace and safety. While they are relaxing after many difficulties and worries. Finally a respite from such challenges and disasters around the world, there is peace at last…then;

Listen to Amos 5:18-20

18Woe to you who long for the Day of the LORD! What will the Day of the LORD be for you? It will be darkness and not light. 19It will be like a man who flees from a lion, only to encounter a bear, or who enters his house and rests his hand against the wall, only to be bitten by a snake. 20Will not the Day of the LORD be darkness and not light, even gloom with no brightness in it?...

---

[73] Isaiah 30:8-11

Just picture a man who escapes from a lion. His heart rate drops after a while and he stops and looks over his shoulder. He relaxes and is very grateful that he was delivered from such a wild animal only to encounter a crazy vicious bear heading or more accurately hurtling straight towards him! Do I dare read a portion of the famous sermon by Jonathan Edwards entitled "Sinners in the hands of an angry God"[74]? This brief excerpt describes the reason for the wrath of God;

Your wickedness makes you as it were heavy as lead, and to tend downwards with great weight and pressure towards hell; and if God should let you go, you would immediately sink and swiftly descend and plunge into the bottomless gulf, and your healthy constitution, and your own care and prudence, and best contrivance, and all your righteousness, would have no more influence to uphold you and keep you out of hell, than a spider's web would have to stop a falling rock. Were it not for the sovereign pleasure of God, the earth would not bear you one moment; for you are a burden to it; the creation groans with you; the creature is made subject to the bondage of your corruption, not willingly; the sun does not willingly shine upon you to give you light to serve sin and Satan; the earth does not willingly yield her increase to satisfy your lusts; nor is it willingly a stage for your wickedness to be acted upon; the air does not willingly serve you for breath to maintain the flame of life in your vitals, while you spend your life in the service of God's enemies. God's creatures are good, and were made for men to serve God with, and do not willingly subserve to any other purpose, and groan when they are abused to purposes so directly contrary to their nature and end. And the world would spew you out, were it not for the sovereign hand of him who hath subjected it in hope. There are the black clouds of God's wrath now hanging directly over your heads, full of the dreadful storm, and big with thunder; and were it not for the restraining hand of God, it would immediately burst forth upon you. The sovereign pleasure of God, for the present, stays his rough wind; other-

---

[74] https://digitalcommons.unl.edu/cgi/viewcontent.cgi?article=1053&context=etas

wise it would come with fury, and your destruction would come like a whirlwind, and you would be like the chaff of the summer threshing floor.
No wonder people jumped out of the church windows!

3. The day of the lord will be impossible to escape from

3 While people are saying, "Peace and safety," destruction will come on them suddenly, as labor pains on a pregnant woman, and they will not escape.

This is not even like when Jonah tried to run from God which he seemingly managed to do for a short period of time! This time some brief running will not be possible. Jonah was being pursued in order to deliver a message of destruction which was like the sandwich board guys message of "repent for the end is near." Amazingly the cruel and nasty city of Nineveh repented in sackcloth and ashes and the disaster was averted. There was no day of visitation yet it was a hint of a greater day. It was a current physical literal reality that pointed to a greater future physical and spiritual dimension.

The great and terrible day of the Lord is only for those who have not repented. It is for the stubborn and the proud but it cannot be prevented, upturned or arrested as it is locked into the schedule so as Isaiah spoke so long ago it is time to get ready!

Isaiah 13

See, the day of the Lord is coming
  —a cruel day, with wrath and fierce anger—
to make the land desolate
  and destroy the sinners within it.
10
The stars of heaven and their constellations
  will not show their light.

> The rising sun will be darkened
> and the moon will not give its light.
> 11
> I will punish the world for its evil,
> the wicked for their sins.
> I will put an end to the arrogance of the haughty
> and will humble the pride of the ruthless.
> 12
> I will make people scarcer than pure gold,
> more rare than the gold of Ophir.
> 13
> Therefore I will make the heavens tremble;
> and the earth will shake from its place
> at the wrath of the Lord Almighty,
> in the day of his burning anger.

The day of the Lord will be sudden though in many ways it has been building for centuries. It will be rapid and unleashed in a torrent as it has been damming up for generations. All tiny spot fires previous were only ever pointing to this day to warn us. It is described in terms of a flood coming on the land, yet not of water this time but of fire and seismic upheaval. It is painted as a time of astronomical calamity, where the planets, the stars, the sun and the moon no longer function as they have done since time immemorial. If even the slightest **astronomical alignment alteration** can cause great tidal movements and extreme weather patterns, and even influence our behaviour, then what will this **complete cosmic chaos** achieve?

Peter quoted Joel as he described the coming of the Holy Spirit yet also pointed to the day of the Lord;

Acts 2:20

> The sun will be turned to darkness and the moon to blood before the coming of the **great and glorious day of the Lord.**

Joel 2:31

The sun will be turned to darkness and the moon to blood before the coming of the **great and dreadful day of the LORD.**

Both authors state that the day will be great yet Joel uses dreadful and Peter uses glorious. The dreadful judgement of God does indeed display his glory and this is a theme throughout the word of God. The difference also reveals where you stand with God. In Peter's day they asked derisively why God is so slow in keeping his promise? He replied in 2 Peter 3:9 that God is not slow in keeping his promise…

9 The Lord is not slow in keeping his promise, as some understand slowness. Instead he is patient with you, not wanting anyone to perish, but everyone to come to repentance.

Paul in Romans 2:4 says something similar when he declares God is just giving us all more chance to repent;

4 Or do you show contempt for the riches of his kindness, forbearance and patience, not realising that **God's kindness** is intended to lead you to repentance?

God is demonstrating great kindness. It is because of the kindness of God that we even have a chance to repent. God has provided a way of escape through the sacrifice of his own beloved son. At great cost he has revealed himself and given up the life of the Holy one for us. It might seem like a 1000 years but to God a 1000 years is just like a day. He is in no rush but he is also not going to delay. The day of the Lord is getting closer all the time.

- Justice is coming…
- Truth is coming…

- The new heaven and earth is coming…
- Perfection is coming….

All that is evil will be judged and removed.
Absolute beauty is on the way but judgement must precede it.
Now is the time to run into the arms of your deliverer.
Don't recklessly hang onto your stubborn and foolish heart.
Allow him to wash you and heal your inner being from sin in order to give you eternal life and escape the coming judgement.
The message that the church must relay to the world truly is "Repent for the day of the Lord is coming!"

The church must be a warning beacon to the world. The day of the Lord is fast approaching as the wrath of God has been building for millennia. It will come without warning and will be in a time of relative security yet there will be no escape.

11

The Children of the Daylight Triplet

The Church is ablaze with light.
AWAKE, SOBER, INVOLVED

1 Thessalonians 5:4-11

The Day of the Lord

4 But you, brothers and sisters, are not in darkness so that this day should surprise you like a thief. **5 You are all children of the light and children of the day. We do not belong to the night or to the darkness.** 6 So then, let us not be like others, who are asleep, but let us be awake and sober. 7 For those who sleep, sleep at night, and those who get drunk, get drunk at night. 8 But since we belong to the day, let us be sober, putting on faith and love as a breastplate, and the hope of salvation as a helmet. 9 For God did not appoint us to suffer wrath but to receive salvation through our Lord Jesus Christ. 10 He died for us so that, whether we are awake or asleep, we may live together with him. 11 Therefore encourage one another and build each other up, just as in fact you are doing.

The Day of the LORD

The day of the Lord is truly God's day. It is the time of the outpouring of divine judgement on sin and sinners. The day of the Lord is not a random physical event whereby the earth on its own accord just starts breaking down as a result of too much human interference or just becoming weary and old! It is the end of the world and for some it truly will be Doomsday. The day of the Lord is the breakdown of all that has functioned like clockwork. Finally the ever dependable sun will be covered "as it were" with sackcloth and the much celebrated pale moon will be cloaked in a blood red garment. The story telling stars in all their constellations will start falling like ripe figs from the branches of the celestial darkness. With the knowledge that an average star is a huge ball of burning gas larger than our sun that becomes a frightening thought! We have to ask why all this should be happening? Why should such catastrophic events be occurring all at once and not separated by millennia according to predictable patterns by eminent astrophysicists? Isaiah outlines the reason as follows;

I will punish the world for its evil,
    the wicked for their sins.
I will put an end to the arrogance of the haughty
    and will humble the pride of the ruthless.[75]

Know this and know it well. This is not the devil's doing, it is most definitely not his day, this is called the day of the Lord and it belongs to no other! It is in truth the final judgement against all the evil one stands for, represents and has built. It is against "the prince of the power of the air" and eventually for all who have been his followers. God has watched the world tear itself apart and it has caused deep pain in his heart. He has held back the vicious violence and hedged it in from getting any

---

[75] Isaiah 13:11

worse than it even is. The lover of our soul has put fences up to prevent Satan from doing any more damage than he has already done and from what he is viciously capable of.

For a brief period of time the word says he will remove these fences.[76] This will be a very tumultuous time for the world. It will be just before the day of the Lord, when the Antichrist has his short-lived but destructive day in the sun. He will then be destroyed in an instant by a single puff of the breath of Christ who returns in glory.[77]

Christians and the Day of the lord

This day need not surprise us although for some that is exactly what will happen! We are being called to live in such a way that we are expecting it and are not caught out. Paul is still speaking in terms of the fusion or confluence between three significant events. He pulls together the second coming to gather Christians along with the day of the Lord to punish sin and sinners as well as the destruction of the present heavens and earth.

Listen to the second verse of 2 Thessalonians 2;

1 Concerning the coming of our Lord Jesus Christ and our being gathered to him, we ask you, brothers and sisters, **2** not to become easily unsettled or alarmed by the teaching allegedly from us—whether by a prophecy or by word of mouth or by letter—asserting that the day of the Lord has already come.

---

[76] **2 Thessalonians 2 :7** For the secret power of lawlessness is already at work; but the one who now holds it back will continue to do so till he is taken out of the way.

[77] 2 Thessalonians 2:8 And then the lawless one will be revealed, whom the Lord Jesus will overthrow with the breath of his mouth and destroy by the splendour of his coming.

The way I read Scripture is that the snatching up, the visible return of Christ to the earth and the day of judgement are all wrapped up together and not to be separated by a complex system of events and dates and times that take away the proximity and the unity of these truths. If there was no proximity such language by Paul makes little sense, especially if Christians had been whisked away at least 1000 years earlier. The verses above in Paul's second letter to the Thessalonians clearly place the coming of Christ and the day of the Lord and even the continued residence of believers on the earth (though about to be taken away) in the exact same time period.

Whenever a preacher speaks on a "controversial topic"[78] he is liable to face a whole range of responses;

- I knew nothing about that so thanks for the teaching
- I have tended to think a bit differently on that issue but I wasn't really sure so that was helpful
- Wow… you're really divisive…. We should just love each other….
- I don't agree but appreciate the fact you used Scripture to back up your arguments
- I stand opposed to everything you just said with all my being… but choose to love you in Christ
- I can't stay in a place where such truths are taught… and we sadly lose a brother or sister…
- Clearly I need to expose you as holding erroneous beliefs as you have obviously just made them up in your own head!

---

[78] This term "controversial" unfortunately has come to mean in some circles anything that our current church thinking isn't too happy with. This could be because of "long held doctrines" or the values we have absorbed from the world. Some of these things though aren't actually very controversial at all! They are rather strong undeniable truths which are essential for church health.

Because of the risk of such things many preachers refuse to preach on such "divisive"[79] topics because they see it as breaking down the unity that exists. The biggest reason though is usually fear of offence and of course the numbers diminishing. How much better it is to have a smaller true church than a church busy with ministries that neglects the heart of God expressed through his word.

God though is into growth and reaching others so don't get me wrong! The book of Acts reveals how much it is truly God's will to reach many others for Christ. What actually happens though is the flock does not get fed, God's people become weak and their spiritual immune system is compromised. The faithful church members can then become people who do not know how to rightly handle scripture. This sets up a scenario whereby Satan can use false teachers to snatch them away or just use the world to entice them as there was no meat being offered. It is important to remember how Jude starts his small letter. He wanted to speak about joyous things such as their salvation but was compelled to warn them against false teaching. He then launches into a scathing attack on "godless dreamers and blemishes" who secretly slip into the flock and do great damage. The world is not afraid to tackle meaty subjects yet they have no reference point other than their own minds or the traditions of those who went before them. We are to be as wise as serpents and as gentle as doves which means the full revealed counsel of God must be thoughtfully preached even if that means treading on some theological toes.

What about the lesson in this passage?

Children of the day… of the light

---

[79] Once again "divisive" has come to mean in "consumer churches" as being anything that threatens the weak and shallow life of a church that has grown by only feeding its people on milk and not meat.

The point clearly enunciated here by Paul is to emphasise that this day need not catch us out by surprise. "This day" as I read Scripture includes the linked and closely connected events of the visible return of Christ, the "being lifted up" of the church, the judgement of sin and sinners and the destruction of the world. It need not catch us out because our identity is now as children of the light even though we used to wander around aimlessly in the darkness. Darkness is about being in a place of sin and ignorance and outside of God and his salvation and his word. Darkness is the realm of the ancient serpent who is the prince of the power of the air.

What is the triplet presented here?

As Children of the day and of the light we are to be the following;

- **Children of the Day are awake**
- **Children of the Day are sober**
- **Children of the Day are involved encouragers**

While we could isolate other dimensions these are the three most significant points in our call to walk as children of the light. As Jesus said just before he raised Lazarus from the dead;

9Jesus answered, "Are there not twelve hours of daylight? If anyone walks in the daytime, he will not stumble, because he sees by the light of this world. 10But if anyone walks at night, he will stumble, because he has no light." [80]

Jesus used a physical example to teach a spiritual truth. If we walk in the light of the Word of God by obedience in the power of the Spirit we will not stumble. If we are frequently watching the metaphorical wheels of our lives come off due to poor choices then we need to repent and come back into the light. We have the power within by the Spirit to turn

---

[80] John 11:9-10

away from the world and its alluring temptations and seek the narrow road which by the way is lit up with the glorious light of Christ. The broad way has many false lights with all sorts of enticing allurements yet is dark, foggy and full of danger. Remember in the old story of Pilgrims Progress that Vanity Fair was very enticing and lulled travellers into a false sense of excitement that promised what it could not deliver. Jesus is the true light in so many ways. The light of the second coming of Christ will be so intense that there will be no need for the sun! Jesus came the first time at night in obscurity and in darkness. He is returning with light so bright that nothing in the physical universe can even begin to compare. Listen to this verse from Zechariah 14 which can be considered as a description of the special and unique nature of this "Day of the Lord."[81]

6 On that day there will be neither sunlight nor cold, frosty darkness. **7** It will be a unique day—a day known only to the Lord—with no distinction between day and night. When evening comes, there will be light.[82]

We sing and affirm that Jesus is the light of the world. When we follow him and refuse to hang onto our sin we also live in light and then we have fellowship with one another as fellowship is especially broken by sin. We are called to live as children of light. The context here is that we know that the end of the world is nigh so we would want to warn others, be pure and holy ourselves and not live for this world that is about to be destroyed by fire. We then live knowing that **"life is short"** but not in the **"carpe diem"**[83] sense of that phrase! In other words we are

---

[81] Here in chapter 14 we have a classic example of Zechariah using many literal physical realities to point to enduring spiritual fulfilment. The language throughout Zechariah is very apocalyptic and Messianic and this continues right to the end of this prophetic book.

[82] Zechariah 14:6-7

[83] Latin for "pluck the day" though usually rendered "seize the day."

to "seize" Christ yet not seize the day for our own gratification and possibly selfish future hopes and dreams. Can we live as if Jesus is coming back in a week, a day or this afternoon? Wouldn't that tire us, exhaust us and make us unreal? Consider someone who has been given a terminal diagnosis, just weeks or months to live, how do they now consider the remaining time that remains?

- All of life is weighed up and reprioritised
- What really matters comes to the fore
- Old pursuits can be tossed aside as if they were rubbish
- New goals can immediately kick in
- Life is suddenly incredibly precious

This is how we can live and we must live like this for this is truly life. This is the way we were supposed to live, in a deep longing for the next world while being full of joy in this broken "about to expire" limited universe. Children of light look to the light of the gospel in the face of Christ. Listen to the Spirit through the Word;

…5For we do not proclaim ourselves, but Jesus Christ as Lord, and ourselves as your servants for Jesus' sake. 6For God, who said, "Let light shine out of darkness," made His light shine in our hearts to give us **the light of the knowledge of the glory of God** in the face of Jesus Christ.[84]

Remember that is how the world was created. At the very beginning there was a powerful entrance of brilliant light and only then was the rest created.

This light of God was made to shine In our hearts, not to remain there but to shine brightly around.

---

[84] 2 Corinthians 4:5-6

This light from Christ through his Spirit gives us spiritual knowledge and understanding. This is so that we can live our lives no longer in the darkness of spiritual ignorance but as children of the day in Christ, whether others understand it or not.

More specifically that knowledge is concerning God's glory. The glory of God is the most important things to live for, to be consumed with, to be caught up in.

So what does this knowledge of the glory of God as revealed in the second coming and the day of the Lord prompt in his children?

1. Children of the Day are awake

There is such a contrast between being awake and asleep, between waking and sleeping; When we are truly asleep we become unaware, ignorant, disengaged and disconnected. Being awake then means being alert, engaged, aware and connected. When you are asleep you are missing out on what is happening, you are in a dream world, in another zone. Being awake means you can make decisions moment by moment and not basically miss out on the big stuff. Matthew 26 tells us when Jesus went away to pray the disciples couldn't keep their eyes open. Jesus on the other hand fell down on the ground crying out to his Father … "if it is possible let this cup pass from me…" we then read;

40Then Jesus returned to the disciples and found them sleeping. "Were you not able to keep watch with Me for one hour?" He asked Peter. 41"Watch and pray so that you will not enter into temptation. For the spirit is willing, but the body is weak."[85]

They were emotionally exhausted, tempted to give in to their bodily needs. Jesus who understands the needs of the body nevertheless calls them to lift above what the body demands. The Spirit is willing, our

---

[85] Matthew 26:40-41

human spirit is willing even, but the body is not able to hold the course on its own. It will fail unless we become truly spiritual people and use the tools we have been given to keep spiritually awake. He calls them to watch and pray in order to not fall into temptation. Watch and pray with me for one hour.

- When you are asleep you are not able to help others
- When you are asleep you are not on the move
- When you are asleep the body is in charge and the spirit does not have the upper hand

This theme is very similar in Ephesians 5 listen to this;

13 But everything exposed by the light becomes visible—and everything that is illuminated becomes a light. **14** This is why it is said: "**Wake up, sleeper**, rise from the dead and Christ will shine on you."

2. Children of the day are sober

The contrast in Ephesians between being drunk on wine and all that follows is with being filled with the Spirit. To put it another way the opposite to being filled with God himself is to be filled with intoxicating spirits of any kind, be they literal or philosophical! The idea in Ephesians 5:18 is to make sure that Christ is in charge and not another ' unclean ' spirit which can be fed by a liquid alcoholic spirit. So the big questions is just who is really in charge? Is our body and its appetites in charge or the Holy Spirit? Just remember that the fruit of the Spirit is self control so when we are tipsy and drunk we can surrender control of our lives to the unholy spirit of liquor. In chapter five of 1 Thessalonians though the idea is more to do with being drunk with the spirit of the world, which might include alcohol, but is by no means limited to it.

This "world drunkenness" will lead to a spiritual stupor that blocks our spiritual sensitivity! We then become "stupefied" and unable to process things properly. It is like being in a marijuana maze or a downer daze or a heroin haze which is not a good place for a Christian to be in. If you drink huge amounts of alcohol while trying to study at University your capacity will be diminished and your results will be affected no matter how hard you might try and study. The capacity to absorb what you are studying decreases as the alcohol consumption increases. All you "Science and Maths lot" reading this would immediately see this very clear inverse relationship!

This is how it is in the spiritual realm yet the "world" spirit is more pervasive and considered by many to be the best on offer. Many say that all that the world dishes up is for our supposed benefit yet it is 100% proof so it will kill us! When it says "spirit of the age" on the bottle label give it a wide berth and run to the Word of God no matter what "vineyard" or "distillery" is doing the production. There are many new "niche distilleries" [86] proudly producing vanity fair produce which we need to be constantly alert to despite the acclaim they might receive by the trendy crew who love to promote the latest diabolical "vintage" on offer.

Listen to John in the second chapter of his first letter…

15 Do not love the world or anything in the world. If anyone loves the world, love for the Father is not in them. **16** For everything in the world—the lust of the flesh, the lust of the eyes, and the pride of life—comes not from the Father but from the world. **17 The world and its desires pass away, but whoever does the will of God lives forever.**

---

[86] To be clear I am referring much more to philosophical and material things than I am to merely alcohol which is neutral in and of itself. I am not against small businesses developing niche products in order to make a living per se. In fact it is a great thing to see creative approaches to business and to see enterprising young and older people giving it a crack!

So instead of a drunken intoxication with the world we instead are called to be sober. This means we refuse to drink huge draughts of what the world has to offer. If we are "hooked" on the world then tell Jesus about it honestly, with tears if we have to and repent. We must then seek to reject the lies the world tells us. The living Christ within has promised to give you the strength. Do this by faith as there is no other way to live in victory. To be sober in Paul's words here in this context then means to learn to drink from the Word of God and the Spirit of God instead of sipping and imbibing at the taverns of the world. These drinking holes might be places of learning, self help books and websites, sporting venues, immoral exploits, created things that are given too high a priority, technology that makes our life more comfortable or many other products in Vanity Fair. James says that friendship with the world makes us an enemy of God. He actually calls them adulterers meaning they love the world more than the lover of their soul.[87] They are unfaithful to Christ as they do not exclusively love God. Taste and see that the Lord is good for he tastes like honey in the rock. The passage continues;

6 So then, let us not be like others, who are asleep, but let us be awake and sober. 7 For those who sleep, sleep at night, and those who get drunk, get drunk at night. 8 But since we belong to the day, let us be sober, putting on faith and love as a breastplate, and the hope of salvation as a helmet.

It is as if Paul is saying we never have a nighttime and as believers that is the way to consider it. We live in the light, we don't spiritually sleep and we don't any longer do what people of the night do. At all times we have the spiritual power by faith to stay sober and remain awake. This is real life and his name is Jesus Christ! He removes depres-

---

[87] James 4:1-8

sion and listlessness and the emptiness we have when we are living for ourselves.

3. Children of the day are involved encouragers

10 He died for us so that, whether we are awake or asleep, we may live together with him. 11 <u>Therefore encourage one another</u> and build each other up, just as in fact you are doing.

In Hebrews we are told to encourage one another and all the more as you see the day approaching.[88]

Inherent in this passage is that one of the ways we actually encourage each other is by meeting together which implies we are having holy fellowship and not just being fellow club attendees. As the day of the Lord gets closer we are told the love of many will grow cold, opposition will heat up and temptations will abound. Paul told Timothy in 1 Timothy 4 that lying spirits will lead people away from the truth;

The Spirit clearly says that in later times some will abandon the faith and follow deceiving spirits and things taught by demons.[89]

We seriously need to encourage each other by speaking truth and firing up a flame of holiness in each other. It is certainly not enough to just be touchy feely, say nice things and always be smiling. All that is superficially fine but true biblical encouragement enables the sheep to stay the course on a narrow path that is fraught with tempting detours. We do this by looking at what Paul said is the way we live in the light, by being awake and sober;

---

[88] Hebrews 10:24 And let us consider how we may spur one another on toward love and good deeds, 25 not giving up meeting together, as some are in the habit of doing, but encouraging one another—and all the more as you see the Day approaching.

[89] I Timothy 4:1

8 But since we belong to the day, let us be sober, putting on faith and love as a breastplate, and the hope of salvation as a helmet.

Faith and Love and Hope, the original triplet, is the way to live the Christian life. There is no other way, therefore it is the way we encourage each other;

- SO….Whenever we are faithless…unbelieving… ungodly…full of doubt
- OR… when we are unloving…harsh…thoughtless…or plain selfish
- OR…when we think of others as hopeless and have no hope for the future ourselves…
- OR…when we are cynical and angry…..
- OR…when we are dismal and despondent all the time…
- We end up discouraging each other and this can result in some of the people of God going off the narrow road and onto tracks in the wilderness that are fraught with danger.

The Church must remain in Christ, knowing his unconditional love at all times, revelling in his grace, and hungering after righteousness so we can be full of faith, hope and love. This then gives us the equipment to encourage others whatever their needs might be.

The Church is called to stay awake at all times. As we remain in a state of readiness we choose to be spiritually sober. We do this by the filling of the Holy Spirit and rejecting all falsehood. Because the day is getting closer we must be involved encouragers of each other so that the Church is holy and effective.

12

The Will of God Triplet

The Church joyfully does the will of God
REJOICE, PRAY, GIVE THANKS

1 Thessalonians 5:16-18

16 Rejoice always, **17** pray continually, **18** give thanks in all circumstances; for this is God's will for you in Christ Jesus.

Big idea… this is not just when we are on holidays, sipping piña coladas and reading our favourite book! Just when do we need to be employing such powerful spiritual tools given to us to be the people of God? The big hint is in the terms "always" and "continually." Let's look at some areas in which the Spirit would remind us to be always be rejoicing, praying and giving thanks;

- when we are in a storm… or when storms collide!
- when we are being buffeted….
- when we can't think straight…
- when we feel like the world has moved on without us…
- when we are desperately lonely….
- when sorrow overwhelms us…
- when loss threatens to undo us…..

What would be the opposite then of what this verse is calling us to do? Perhaps more accurately what would be the common, human, understandable way to respond to multiple knocks and mistreatment?

- Be overwhelmed and depressed always.
- Madly scramble to work everything ourselves.
- Blame God and everyone else for the mess we are in.

To summarise this we might say the following would be a pretty common way to respond;

- Anxiously groan
- Fearfully strive
- Bitterly blame

Perhaps even more succinctly we could fall into;

- Depression
- Fear
- Bitterness

In other words when we are tempted to groan, panic and blame we can choose by faith to rejoice, pray and give thanks!

The Context is when we are undergoing really tough stuff or in other words when life is just way too hard.

THE WILL OF GOD

Now let's actually get to the real immediate context which is about how to do the will of god in Christ Jesus as that is what the verse actually says. How do we truly do what God wants when life is taking a turn for the worst? We can learn to be so free that we no longer groan, panic and blame! We can instead discover how to rejoice, pray and be thankful. Only in the will of God are we free and able to impact others.

THE NATURE OF SORROW

Does this mean we can never feel pain, grief, sorrow and anguish? Before we go any further the answer is a resounding NO but we do need to address the false teaching that rises up around this verse and all sorts of wacky associated ideas. It is incredibly important we remember that Jesus was known as "a man of sorrows, acquainted with grief." Let's not pass over that too quickly. Please read this verse slowly allowing the reality of what Christ went through to sink in because as he is in the world so are we;

He was despised and rejected by men, a man of sorrows, acquainted with grief. Like one from whom men hide their faces, He was despised, and we esteemed Him not.[90]

In other words to rejoice does not mean we don't pass through deep valleys of grief. It just means we do both at he same time. We may have deep sorrow yet also we choose to rejoice in the midst of the sorrow. The nature of rejoicing then must be carefully considered. You may not

---

[90] Isaiah 53:3 BSB

be happy on the surface because of untold sorrow or persecution but we can rejoice in Christ with the sorrow. It doesn't have to make sense with our earthly perspective but it is how God has designed things to work. He has passed through such waters and he is present with us even now.

- Being real isn't being stuck in sorrow with no rejoicing
- Being spiritual doesn't mean cutting off sorrow and suffering as if they weren't part and parcel of the human experience.
- We must walk with sorrow and suffering along with learning to rejoice.
- We rejoice in our sorrows.
- We may walk alone yet rejoice, pray and give thanks.

WHAT'S FAITH GOT TO DO WITH IT?

Faith is the key to all of this yet perhaps not in the way that some preachers so loudly emphasise. Some of us have sadly given up on faith because someone said to us we didn't have enough of it when we were in a world of grief. Please don't let an insensitive approach block you from a key aspect of truth behind their words. The reality is there is no progress or advancement in the Kingdom of God unless we do truly get what faith is. It is that important! We are frozen and fruitless and foggy without faith! FAITH is based on knowing **who God really is** and **how much he and his word can be trusted.**

- Just how much does he see my dilemma?
- What can he do about it?
- How much does he want to do anything about it?

Reflect briefly on Hagar whose story is in Genesis 16 and 21. She discovered that the Lord is "the God who sees." She called God "El Roi" which means the God who sees because he didn't just see;

- He looked with compassion
- He powerfully intervened to bring a blessing
- He called Hagar by name.

El Roi in his divine plan even called her to return for at least 14 years to the very people who had treated her poorly. She was then kicked out a second time and once again God intervened and blessed her and her son Ishmael. He grew to become a powerful leader of a man. You would not want to have crossed him as he was going to become "…a wild donkey of a man."[91] FAITH then is seeing the invisible God with our mind's eye or more precisely the eyes of our heart.[92] FAITH is rising up into a stratum that is above this earth in the spiritual realm. We learn to not live by the terror of the circumstances we are surrounded by but by the promises in the Word of God. This is faith.

We live by FAITH Not by SIGHT so therefore …

Instead of despairing we rejoice, pray and give thanks in all things.

IMPOSSIBLE NATURE OF THESE THREE DIRECTIVES

These three wonderful sounding bible terms (Rejoice, Pray and Give thanks) are humanly impossible. Our sinful nature can't actually do this triplet. It is impossible, unrealistic and could even be deceitful if we pretend we can on our own. Our reality is sometimes just "too much for us to handle" so why such an apparently heartless directive? Not only that, we are so naturally weak we can't completely follow any holy commands of any kind. Our every attempt to do so is weakened by the flesh. We sadly just aren't able to keep the law of God. It's not just that we don't

---

[91] Gen 16:12

[92] Ephesians 1:18 I pray that the eyes of your heart may be enlightened in order that you may know the hope to which he has called you, the riches of his glorious inheritance in his holy people,

like being told what to do, we actually cannot do what the commands say. Have a read of the following powerful teaching in Romans which describes this complete inability to be the people of God on our own;

1 Therefore, there is now no condemnation for those who are in Christ Jesus, 2 because through Christ Jesus the law of the Spirit who gives life has set you free from the law of sin and death. **3 For what the law was powerless to do because it was weakened by the flesh**, God did by sending his own Son in the likeness of sinful flesh to be a sin offering. And so he condemned sin in the flesh, **4 in order that the righteous requirement of the law might be fully met in us, who do not live according to the flesh but according to the Spirit.**[93]

This raises the crucial and sometimes forgotten question as to what the authentic Christian life really is all about. Something clearly had to change for holiness to be possible so just what did change between the covenants?

JESUS CAME…!

He did what we couldn't do for ourselves and that changes everything! The bible describes 2 main ways that we must constantly choose between that lie deep within us. They are forces that fight against each other. This sums up the difference between the two covenants. It is about the source of our spiritual life and the chief goal of that life. It answers the question of how we do the will of God. How do we live for the Messiah under the New Covenant? It also reveals to the church how to build on a foundation that is truly from a heavenly blueprint and repent from a contemporary consumer mentality.

---

[93] Romans 8:1-4

LAW vs SPIRIT

In the Old Testament, let's say from Exodus onwards, we find that Law is the direction to head and the source of power. In other words if you do this holy commandment and work at that divine directive you shall live. What a wonderful life purpose lies in this body of commands and precepts that flow from the very nature of the Holy one. We are even told the precepts of the Lord are forever. Here are the commands we are told so now go and do them and life will flow like a river. David frequently said how amazing the law of God is in many different ways and it truly is. The only issue was that they and subsequently every person desiring to do the will of God discovered it was just way too hard. Something kept getting in the way and that something is our flesh, called the sinful nature or the old person. Our working (works) to keep the Law (obedience) just did not produce the life (holiness) that pleases God.

THEN JESUS CAME...

Under the New Covenant in the blood of Christ we find that Jesus did what we could not do. He fulfilled completely the Law right down to [as the KJV says] the last "jot and tittle." Here it is in more contemporary English;

17"Do not think that I have come to abolish the Law or the Prophets. I have not come to abolish them, but to fulfill them. 18For I tell you truly, until heaven and earth pass away, not a single jot, not a stroke of a pen, will disappear from the Law until everything is accomplished."[94]

Jesus did totally fulfil the Law and "everything was accomplished" or in Jesus own word on the cross in Greek "tetelestai" which means it

---

[94] Matthew 5:17,18 BSB

is finished, it is fulfilled, it is completed. We are now no longer bound to the law but free in the one who fulfilled the law on our behalf due to our inability do so. The life we now live is by the Spirit instead of by the law. It is by faith instead of works. It always looks to Jesus instead of our own efforts. So, the Spirit by faith gives us life and power to be like Christ making our goal now to be a person who is the perfect son of God. That is why we must constantly be filled with the Spirit in order to be like Christ. To do what Jesus does and says by the Spirit of Christ now becomes our goal. This leads to holiness and power and is called by Paul in the introduction to the letter to the Romans the obedience that comes from faith. [95] Loving his word and obeying it flows from faith and looking to Christ. We then fulfil the law of liberty as the law of the OT is already fulfilled in us by the only one who can ever obey perfectly. It is faith or the law…The Spirit or works. Paul describes this inner tussle as follows;

16 So I say, walk by the Spirit, and you will not gratify the desires of the flesh. 17 For the flesh desires what is contrary to the Spirit, and the Spirit what is contrary to the flesh. They are in conflict with each other, so that you are not to do whatever you want. **18 But if you are led by the Spirit, you are not under the law.**[96]

Law is a set of principles that are right and good. It is a great and godly direction to be driving toward. Obedience to the principles is through our will power and commitment and drive and surrender to God. This is a call to righteousness, to holiness, yet it is impossible due to our sinful natures and it is weakened by the flesh so we fail and fall, drenched in guilt and shame.

---

[95] 5 Through him we received grace and apostleship to call all the Gentiles to **the obedience that comes from faith** for his name's sake.

[96] Galatians 5:16-18

The law, though it is holy, is tied to our flesh and the flesh ends up sinning all the time. We have to die to the law for the flesh to no longer have such power. This dying to the law is biblically described in the following way;

4 So, my brothers and sisters, you also **died to the law** through the body of Christ, that you might belong to another, to him who was raised from the dead, in order that we might bear fruit for God. **5** For when we were in the realm of the flesh, the sinful passions aroused by the law were at work in us, so that we bore fruit for death. **6 But now, by dying to what once bound us, we have been released from the law so that we serve in the new way of the Spirit, and not in the old way of the written code.**[97]

For example the psalmist asks the age old question as how a young man can live a pure life? Here is the answer given;

9How can a young man keep his way pure?
By guarding it according to Your word.
10With all my heart I have sought You;
do not let me stray from your commandments.
11I have hidden Your word in my heart
that I might not sin against You.[98]

The Old Testament has the Word of God and his commands as the basis for holiness as this is both THE SOURCE AND THE GOAL.

Spirit living is entirely different though, it is a new way, a new covenant. Jesus did what we couldn't do. He fulfilled the perfect requirements of the law as he was the only ever truly pure young man as described in Psalm 119... the very first! The bible says all young men have sinned that means Joseph and Elijah and Moses and Noah even!

---

[97] Romans 7:4-6
[98] Psalm 119:9-11

We died to the law to live for Christ and we can't have both! He also took the guilt of our sin, our failure to be obedient to the law, our unholiness, onto the cross. He became sin that we might become the righteousness of God and this is the gospel. He became the final sacrifice for our failure to obey the law. So, what's that go to do with our reading today? We must not read this as just 3 new commands, as just 3 new laws. The New Covenant is not just swapping one set of laws for another. If we did this the standard would be even higher. It is even harder to do what is right so we may as well just be hypocrites as God is true but we have no hope of ever doing what he wants. This is instead a call to be holy in the Spirit. An invitation to live life in the Spirit. A summons to do what we cannot do on our own. In its most profound sense it is a heavenly provision to do what formerly could not be done. You see, the law is based on works which means do this and you will live, you will be holy, you will please God, you will do the will of God. Life in the Spirit looks to JESUS by Faith as having done all such things already and then by faith we live in his power. He lives out his own life in us in order for us to be like him. Before we were "under law" now we are "in Christ" and there is a very big difference. It is all about the power source and the one fulfilled life and both are found in the Son of God. Life in the SPIRIT means we are already made holy…

- already justified….
- already accepted…
- already a fully fledged member of the royal heavenly family….
- already this is all done for us…
- Time to live in the "already" instead of waiting for what has now come.

Our righteousness doesn't come from doing these three amazing things or any other Christian activity or any obedience to the law as it is all by faith. Read what Paul says to build up the church in Philippi;

...8More than that, I count all things as loss compared to the surpassing excellence of knowing Christ Jesus my Lord, for whom I have lost all things. I consider them rubbish, that I may gain Christ **9and be found in Him, not having my own righteousness from the law, but that which is through faith in Christ, the righteousness from God on the basis of faith.**[99]

This produces an amazing freedom so much so that Paul says... now... be careful with this freedom ! Do not use your freedom to indulge the Flesh!

13 You, my brothers and sisters, were called to be free. **But do not use your freedom to indulge the flesh**; rather, serve one another humbly in love.[100]

It is time to examine the triplet

16 Rejoice always, **17** pray continually, **18** give thanks in all circumstances; for this is God's will for you in Christ Jesus.

1. Rejoice always

What does this even really mean? It is such a churchy word that we can miss out on the power of this truth, this practice, this directive. Firstly just what is the Kingdom of Heaven about?

For the kingdom of God is not a matter of eating and drinking, but of righteousness, peace and joy in the Holy Spirit...Romans 14:17

Whatever rejoicing is it is very much a component of belonging to the Kingdom. God wants us to be filled with joy but how can we when

---

[99] Philippians 3:8-9
[100] Galatians 5:13

things are a mess? Here we find a heavenly antidote to a problem that the world will never understand. What God has for us is the opposite to what the world holds out. His will is the solution to groaning and depression, to overcoming a pessimistic outlook and to getting victory over weighty burdens that are thrown at us. Isaiah described the work of the Messiah and much later Jesus declared in his home town that this prophecy was about him;

1 The Spirit of the Lord GOD is on Me, because the LORD has anointed Me to preach good news to the poor. He has sent Me to bind up the brokenhearted, to proclaim liberty to the captives and freedom to the prisoners, 2 to proclaim the year of the LORD's favor and the day of our God's vengeance, to comfort all who mourn, **3 to console the mourners in Zion—to give them a crown of beauty for ashes, the oil of joy for mourning, and a garment of praise for a spirit of despair.** So they will be called oaks of righteousness, the planting of the LORD, that He may be glorified[101]

Beauty for ashes, the **oil of joy for mourning** and the garment of praise for a spirit of despair or heaviness. This is a supernatural, divine gift from above. Do you long to have real inner beauty, a liberal dose of the oil of joy and to be wrapped up in a garment of praise? It takes us out of a "normal" way of living and lifts us to a place that the world cannot know.

The Greek Word Chairo (rejoice) is closely related to Chara (joy) and Charis (Grace).

To <u>rejoice</u> then is to make a faith choice that takes us out of despair and <u>leads us to joy.</u> This in itself is an act of worship.

When the wise men continued their search for the Messiah they saw the star;

---

[101] Isaiah 61:1-3

9After they had heard the king, they went on their way, and the star they had seen in the east went ahead of them until it stood over the place where the Child was. 10When they saw the star, they **rejoiced with great delight.** 11On coming to the house, they saw the Child with His mother Mary, and they fell down and worshipped Him. Then they opened their treasures and presented Him with gifts of gold and frankincense and myrrh. [102]

Getting closer to Jesus enables us to rejoice with great delight as the very heart of our inner searching is finally found. So how do we enter into this incredibly unnatural response to tragedy, sorrow and attacks be they verbal or otherwise? It is always and only ever a faith choice by the Spirit. This is not a fleeting happiness just based on how well things are turning out.

Whatever we might have lost… we have Christ… who is the pearl of great price… the wisdom of the ages… the rose of Sharon…the balm of Gilead… the lover of our soul… the judge of the whole earth… the Shepherd of the sheep.

As we choose to rejoice in every overwhelming difficulty a change comes over our demeanour and we are lifted;

12Beloved, do not be surprised at the fiery trial that has come upon you, as though something strange were happening to you. **13But rejoice that you share in the sufferings of Christ, so that you may be overjoyed at the revelation of His glory.** 14If you are insulted for the name of Christ, you are blessed, because the Spirit of glory and of God rests on you[103]

This may seem very strange in some ways in the midst of a terrible thing happening to us but it is a way ahead. To know you are actually sharing in the sufferings of Christ is very special as in this world we are

---

[102] Matthew 2:9-11
[103] 1 Peter 4:13

like him. We can **"rejoice"** in difficulty as this builds us up in the here and now yet it points to the future experience of being **"overjoyed"** at the revelation of his glory when he returns.

In other words how do we truly get ready for Jesus return? By rejoicing when we suffer as we are then entering into the sufferings of Christ who died to give us joy. It leads us to a place where **our identification with him** is so great that when he returns we will be not just vindicated, not just be dramatically changed, we will also be overjoyed and full of incredible delight as we have been like him.

2. Pray continually

The word for "continually" can't be really undercut or diminished.

It means constantly, incessantly and with no unnecessary intervals.

In other words having hardly any time gap between what is being discussed which in this case is "praying sessions." There are surely many dimensions of prayer and this is what Paul undoubtedly means. Here are just a few;

> Petition…being impressed to intercede for another
> Presence…practicing the presence of God
> Protection ….knowing Christ as our fortress and rock
> Providence… being at peace as God is in total control

Cultivating a sense of the presence of God proceeds from a dual understanding of being set free from the guilt and power of our sin and the curse of the law as well as living daily in the Spirit unto holiness. We do this by being filled with the Spirit daily in order to be like Christ. This is what Jesus spoke about when he said we are to be at all times connected to the vine, to abide in him and not try and survive on our own if we want to thrive. The conscious decision to do so stimulates us to consider the needs of others. We petition God for their benefit, for their growth so that the eyes of their hearts will be enlightened.

While we live under a cloud of condemnation though we will be less inclined or able to engage in such an activity. It is out of our freedom that we learn to pray continually, to breath heavenly air, to live by faith and to stand against the temptations of the world. Choosing to live by the Spirit and not under law leads us into the presence of Christ as there is no condemnation to those in Christ Jesus. Prayer is not so much an angry desperate… "you better do something or I'll never talk to you again" but a deepening of the divine relationship which Christ himself has initiated.

What then is a fuller description of prayer?

- aligning ourselves with the will of God…
- repenting of sin…
- submitting to his will…
- longing for a closer walk…
- trusting and waiting…
- praising and worshipping the Holy one…
- Being filled with him.

If our prayers never alter then we are not being changed by the process of prayer which is the call to be in the presence of the holy one. It is allowing him to direct the situation knowing he is sovereign and loves us more than we can ever know. The amazing thing is as we pray with listening ears[104] he reveals more of the situation to us.

3. Give Thanks in all circumstances

This power tool is perhaps the toughest of all in "the natural".

---

[104] Isaiah 50:4 The Sovereign Lord has given me a well-instructed tongue, to know the word that sustains the weary. He wakens me morning by morning, wakens my ear to listen like one being instructed.

We must remember though the impossibility of this triplet and the natural pull back to being the broken old person whereby we exhibit the following symptoms;

- Anxiously groan
- Fearfully strive
- Bitterly blame

Shifting away from the need to blame

So firstly instead of "bitterly blame" we live in the power of the Spirit to instead give thanks in all circumstances. How easy it is to "look for someone to blame…" as it is the natural operation of the flesh. Frequently though we can end up seeing things that are not even there in order to find such a "blameworthy" person.

In some cultures the need to "finish a matter by payback or revenge" is very strong. Unfortunately this is considered in terms of justice which is not an equivalent idea. The resolution to a difficult, sad or horrific situation in such a mindset is just to punish someone severely which in the end leaves us wounded ourselves. Our inner drive to get revenge can amazingly be replaced by the Spirit of God enabling us to "…give thanks in all circumstances." When we remain in our old selves all we see is the loss, the injustice and the pain. So many movies are based on a blind rage being acted out by a hurt person who is "hell bent" on revenge. This is not just restricted to the movies though as we all know very well. As we come to Christ and walk with the man of sorrows we can learn to thank him for the things that no-one can ever take away.

What can we thank God for…?

We are his sheep, we are children of the Father, we have access to the throne room of grace every moment of the day and night, we have an eternal dwelling reserved for us, we have the righteousness of God from

God apart from the law given to us and there is much more. We have our deepest needs met at a level that no earthly person or thing can ever do.

Focussing on the spiritual and eternal things that are forever will change our limited earthly temporal perspective on a matter. This is why Paul is so strong about describing the spiritual blessings in Christ in the early part of his letter to the Ephesian church. Now remember we do these three things in order to do the will of God. We are reminded in the verse that we are in Christ otherwise the doing of these three things is impossible.

Looking back to remind ourselves of the Grace of God

Secondly we give thanks because whenever we get an answer to prayer we can immediately be buffeted by the next problem. How easy it is to forget to thank God for how he has helped us so far. To deliberately look back and remind ourselves of all the ways God has both answered our actual prayers and helped us when we haven't even asked him is so crucial for our spiritual development and protection. In the Old Testament this principle of actively choosing to set up a permanent reminder of the goodness of God is known as the Ebenezer stone. At one time Samuel calls upon God's people to be genuine in their repentance by turning from their idols with their whole heart. He then worships by offering a burnt offering of a young lamb. It is at this point that the devil who hates repentance and worship stirs up the Philistines and causes them to mount an attack. We then read that as they cried out to the Lord he "thundered with a great thunder"[105] and routed the enemy. They chased the mighty army and won such a victory that the Philistines did not bother them for a very long time. Samuel then sets up a stone of remembrance stating "thus far has the Lord helped us"[106] calling it "Ebenezer"

---

[105] 1 Samuel 7:10
[106] 1 Samuel 7:12

which means "stone of help" in Hebrew. Ingratitude is a malignant spiritual disease. It threatens to wipes us out and makes us vulnerable. Give thanks in all things. We don't give thanks for the actual horrific loss or sad situation but for the way God is at work despite what the devil has been trying to achieve. There is an old saying that roughly goes like "God reaps his best crops in the paddocks that Satan has ploughed!"

The often quoted verse in Romans then begins to make sense;

And we know that God causes all things to work together for good to those who love God, to those who are called according to His purpose.[107]

The church has a heart of obedience which is expressed in doing completely the will of God. The people of God are characterised by rejoicing in suffering, praying when burdened and thankful in all things at all times.

---

[107] Romans 8:28

Let's finish this chapter with a famous song by Robert Robinson that has reference to the Ebenezer stone of remembrance.

1. Here I raise my Ebenezer,
Hither by thine help I've come;
And I hope, by thy good pleasure,
Safely to arrive at home.

2. Jesus sought me, when a stranger,
Wandering from the fold of God,
He, to rescue me from danger,
Interposed with precious blood.

3. O! to grace, how great a debtor
Daily I'm constrained to be!
Let thy goodness, like a fetter,
Bind my wandering heart to thee.

13

Body, Soul and Spirit Triplet

The Church is holistic
SPIRIT, SOUL, BODY

---

1 Thessalonians 5:23, 24

23Now may the **God of peace** Himself sanctify you completely, and may your entire **spirit, soul, and body** be kept blameless at the coming of our Lord Jesus Christ. 24The One who calls you is faithful, and He will do it.

One of the self revealed names of God is "the God of Peace." Gideon uses this name for God when he calls an altar he builds "Jehovah Shalom" once he realises he has seen the holy angel of the Lord and has been spared. It is the divine plan to keep us in a place of being guarded by his peace that goes beyond reason and instead is said to transcend understanding. These verses are the pathway to peace, to rest, to finally relinquish being churned up and tossed around within our inner being, in essence to find tranquility.

Now may the God of Shalom [108] lead you to that place of deep rest and integrity. May he do this by leading us to a place of holiness and purity and being kept blameless.

This prayer is inherently also a promise and shows us he can do it, he wants to do it and he is faithful to do it! It is a call to trust Christ. He deals with the whole of our being which means right down to the deepest parts, to the inner hidden person which is only known by the one who has knit us together in our mother's womb. This whole person is described as being spirit, soul and body.

- We are more than just a body no matter how strong our bodily impulses may be.
- We are more than just a soul which is that inner part whereby all people feel and think and choose.
- We also have a spirit through which the Holy Spirit speaks and directs and fills us.

What is the distinction between the spirit, the soul and the body?

AT THE CREATION

Then the LORD God formed a man from the dust of the ground and breathed into his nostrils the breath of life, and the man became a living being. Genesis 2:7 NIV

We were created with a body as a living being ...a "nephesh" in Hebrew. The formation of a "Nephesh" occurred when we were breathed upon with his breath, his Spirit, and then governed by the Spirit of God through the human spirit. The spirit and soul operated as one and the body cooperated in a perfect synchrony. I believe this to be a biblically

---

[108] Shalom: Hebrew word for peace meaning rest and complete inner wholeness. It is a holistic state of blessedness.

comprehensive way to describe Genesis 2:7 when we take into account the rest of Scripture. Many though feel with substantial biblical underpinning that there is no distinction between spirit and soul. I will be briefly touching on this debate in the remainder of this chapter as there are many good reasons why such a distinction is spiritually helpful. God shared his life with Adam in the deepest part of his being. He was created in the image of God in order to know and love God and also to humbly govern the earth. God is spirit and we must worship him in spirit and in truth. We are not taught that God is "soul" which may seem a small point but it is very important.

All was beautiful and perfect.

All was at peace and at rest until the big crash.

THEN THE FALL

If you eat this fruit you shall die…!

This directive followed from… "enjoy all the fruit in the garden except for this one fruit alone. Do not eat that one fruit or you shall die…" [109]

In Chapter 3 the serpent asked a very tricky question;

"Did God say you may not eat from ANY tree in the garden…?"

Eve responded to the serpent by adding "and not even touch the fruit "of the one forbidden tree. This embellishment of the truth opened the door to having doubt cast like a dark shadow on the goodness of God. The woman and the man both ate and in one cataclysmic blow the spirit part of a human being was cut off from God. The previously

---

[109] **Genesis 2:15** The Lord God took the man and put him in the Garden of Eden to work it and take care of it. **16** And the Lord God commanded the man, "You are free to eat from any tree in the garden; **17** but you must not eat from the tree of the knowledge of good and evil, for when you eat from it you will certainly die."

sinless couple were suddenly unable to understand the deep spiritual truths that formerly came so easily. They ceased to be able to hear the Holy Spirit, the things of heaven, in order to live properly here on earth. In the language of John they could no longer hear the voice of the Good Shepherd. As we are in solidarity with our first parents[110] according to Romans we too became "dead in our transgressions and sins."[111] The big question then is "what actually died?"

I believe the spirit part of us fell asleep as if it was in a spiritual coma. The human spirit prior to the new birth is now considered as dead, effectively cut off from God and unable to hear his voice. We become disconnected to the environment both of heaven and in many ways even of the earth. Due to the sin of our first parents we are then born with our spirit being dead in spiritual terms. Our only alternative now is to be guided by our soul. This is a route which has been described by Watchman Nee as being "soulish."[112] This is because we are now guided by that part of us which came from the earth and therefore only can receive from below. We could call this broken and incomplete manner of being "earthy" and is very open to the tempting and deceiving work of Satan. This swings our attention to the Greek term ψυχικός 'Psuchikos' which comes from the Greek word for soul… Psuche (soo-ke). Psuchikos (soo-ki-kos) is often translated as sensual, worldly or fleshly. That is why it would be most helpful if in English we had a word like … "soulish" …which could then mean pertaining to the earth. The sinful nature (the old self) also called the flesh which is itself being corrupted day by day though its own deceitful desires now acts upon the soul and controls it. The intention of this "root of sin" is to govern the body and drag it down causing it be earthy and sensual and unholy, in essence directed away from God.

---

[110] Romans 5:12-15

[111] Ephesians 2:1

[112] Collected Works of Watchman Nee, The (Set 1) Vol. 12: The Spiritual Man (1)

BEING BORN AGAIN

Only in Christ can we experience new life through the Spirit in our "now awake" human spirit. We are born from above as Jesus explained to Nicodemus in John 3:3. [113] We are awakened in our spirit and finally able to hear from God. Finally the connection is re-established. If you like the static is now replaced by a clear signal as the transmitter and receiver are hooked up correctly once again.

At last the way back to the God of love and justice is restored. This reconciliation is through believing that the wages of sin is death: both spiritual and biological. It is through believing that the price was paid for our sin by the perfect sacrifice of the Son of God;

He died the death we deserved.
He rose again and gave us his new life
Our spirit is now alive… awake… vibrant… true… vital!

This new life is by the perfect life of Christ being mysteriously united with our spirit and bringing life which is by faith. The ancient long sought for path toward heaven and therefore to wholeness had now been revealed. Unfortunately though the initial act of the new birth doesn't mean we are immediately free from the grip of the deep root of sin while we still occupy these earthly bodies. We must daily receive the filling of the Holy Spirit in order to receive life from above into our human spirit. If we are not daily filled with this golden spiritual oil we become "born again yet broken." This results in an ugly hypocrisy and self deceit with the subsequent lack of harvest in the fields of the kingdom of God which are ripe for harvest to the one in tune with the Spirit. The awakened spirit requires the Holy Spirit to truly have the desire, the power and the knowledge as to how to live for God.

---

[113] **3** Jesus replied, "Very truly I tell you, no one can see the kingdom of God unless they are born again."

The Spirit acts upon our spirit to flood into the soul…purifying it…and to direct the body and hence our whole being upward in a holy manner…toward God himself.

So the battle is between the flesh and the Spirit over who controls the soul of a man and therefore the expression of the body unto God. This is a daily battle that will not diminish until either we die or Christ returns in glory. Daily we are given strength for the journey, forgiveness for failures and hidden manna for our inner being. As we feed on Christ himself we remain joined to him in a mystical and glorious way. All of this is by faith. Watchman Nee words it as follows;

It is imperative that a believer knows he has a spirit, since, as we shall soon learn, every communication of God with man occurs there. If the believer does not discern his own spirit he invariably is ignorant of how to commune with God in the spirit. He easily substitutes the thoughts or emotions of the soul for the works of the spirit. Thus he confines himself to the outer realm, unable ever to reach the spiritual realm.[114]

Why isn't life a breeze after salvation?

Once we are born again and our spirit is awake it would appear that all things should be smooth sailing from that point? Shouldn't it?

We find a hint in the following verse as to why this is not the case;

…13 And this is what we speak, not in words taught us by human wisdom, but in words taught by the Spirit, expressing spiritual truths in spiritual words. 14 **The natural man** does not accept the things that come from the Spirit of God. For they are foolishness to him, and he cannot understand them, because they are spiritually discerned. 15 **The spiritual man** judges all things, but he himself is not subject to anyone's judgment.[115]

---

[114] Collected Works of Watchman Nee, The (Set 1) Vol. 12: The Spiritual Man (1)
[115] 1 Corinthians 2:13-14

In other words these things are spiritually understood and our "natural" flesh is still very much in operation. If we try and do this christian bit on our own then look out or we'll run into deep problems!

It is most accurate biblically to say that the struggle we face is between the "soulish" man vs the spiritual man. This struggle is not possible for unbelievers as their spirit is still in a comatose state and is effectively dead. This conflict is only in the life of the child of God, not the one who is spiritually asleep. Many people dead in their spirits yet awake to the dark arts describe their activity as spiritual yet it is actually evil spirits acting on their souls and bringing all sorts of lies and arguments against the love of God. Most of what is termed spiritual by the world is in fact "external evil spirits" operating at a soul level as opposed to the Holy Spirit flowing through our regenerated human spirits and then producing sanctified souls. In that regard only a born again believer can actually be spiritual as all other activity then becomes occultish or at least "soulish".

Hence Paul prays;

23Now may the God of peace Himself sanctify you completely, and may your **entire spirit, soul, and body** be kept blameless at the coming of our Lord Jesus Christ.

It is all about what we come to rely on. We can have a born again, awakened spirit yet still be depending on the familiar natural, soulish way of living and not be Spirit dependent. A key determiner of this is how much we allow the Word to transform our thinking. The "soulish" or worldly Christian still operates from his earthy soul, formed from the dust, from the earth. Such a person is reluctant to allow the Word of God to completely fill their minds and will be searching for other inputs as they are dissatisfied with God's word seeing it as somehow incomplete or even antiquated. This can also be easily determined as there is no peace in our hearts. Just as the earth is constantly changing and being made unstable so is the soulish person. In 1955 an article appeared in the Norwegian periodical called "Hidden Treasures" which described vividly what is going on;

"Everything that is of the earth is unsteady and changeable, which is why a person who allows their soul to control their life is never at rest. Through the soul – through my senses and feelings – I am in contact with people. Someone who lives according to the soul is always in unrest with regard to what other people think and say about him."[116]

The spiritual person looks to God for their life and wisdom and direction and he is a God of peace. If we have no peace we are probably being driven from the soul, not the spirit. It is a constant necessity for our lamps to be filled with the calming oil of the Spirit. This is done through the human spirit being awake constantly to the things of Christ and being alert to the traps and tricks of Satan. Watchman Nee states that a "soulish" person will tend to depend upon themselves in the 3 ways that a soul functions. Let's carefully examine these three mechanisms according to Watchman Nee whereby we can be "soulish" (soul in charge and content to not seek help from above) instead of spiritual (spirit in charge and directing the soul toward the Word of God having received from the Holy Spirit).

"THE INTELLECTUAL."

Controlled by the mind

The intellect is paramount and thinking is proud

Very interested in intellectual things
Research is primary

---

[116] This is an edited version of an article that was first published in Norwegian under the title "Pierces and divides soul from spirit" in BCC's periodical Skjulte Skatter (Hidden Treasures) in August 1955.

Proud of their capacity to think and reason things through
Weighing up choices is more important than prayer
God's revelation is less important than brainstorming and "putting our heads together."

"THE HEDONIST."

Contolled by the emotions

They are hedonistic or experience run

Sensations and strong emotions are preferred over raw and tough faith
Bursts of feeling are highly sought after
Life is not real without these mountaintop experiences
God cannot be speaking without throbbing emotion…so is ignored

Watchman Nee describes such a person;

> *"Those who are soulish usually thrive on sensation. The Lord affords them the sense of His presence before they attain spirituality. They treat such a sensation as their supreme joy. When granted such a feeling, they picture themselves as making huge strides towards the peak of spiritual maturity. Yet the Lord alternately bestows and withdraws this touch that He might gradually train them to be weaned from sensation and walk by faith. These do not understand the way of the Lord, however, and conclude that their spiritual condition is highest when they can feel the Lord's presence and lowest when they fail to do so."*[117]

This speaks to the consumer contemporary church in a way that brings a strong rebuke. Are we people of faith or do we crave sensation before the will of God? The consumer church seeks out emotional experiences before the life of daily sacrifice and surrender that is char-

---

[117] Collected Works of Watchman Nee, The (Set 1) Vol. 12: The Spiritual Man (1)

acterised by Emmanuel. Such a seemingly vibrant church may find the Christ with his nailed pierced hands knocking repeatedly on the door and wonder who such a sorrowful looking man could be.[118]

"THE LONE REBEL."

Controlled by the will

Convinced of the path they have set themselves by their own wisdom they rush ahead.

At the heart of a soulish christian is wilfulness

Nobody can tell me what to do

They do not understand that self denial is at the heart of being a follower of Christ.

They can be "free spirits" who cannot be tied to any set path or direction. The Word of God says such rebellion is as witchcraft. [119]

Alternatively they can be very disciplined and hard working people yet unwilling to be influenced by godly people who seek to speak into their lives as they have their will set and will not be altered.

All of this leads to one big disaster spiritually.

Yet it is right here where the "real rubber hits the road" begins to kick in. It is right here where churches either continue as "soulish" in their endeavours or become truly spiritual. Operating as a church in such a worldly way may look amazing to other "soulish" christians who have loved the activity, the discussion, the reasoning, the inclusion and other such corporate activities. Any attempt to lead people back into the

---

[118] Revelation 3:20

[119] For rebellion is like the sin of divination, and arrogance is like the wickedness of idolatry. 1 Sam 15:23. BSB

Word of God will be seen as authoritarian, old fashioned and horrifyingly not inclusive. Such immature believers fail to recognise that dying to self and the transformation of the new self by the Word of God is the most important activity of a Christian, not the promotion of the old self. It is once again either a choice to follow the inner pull to "finding myself" and having my opinions validated or by faith to choose to "lose oneself for the sake of Christ" and be submitted to his word. The person who dies to self ends up discovering that they have the greatest treasure of all and they are complete in a way that any "self searching" can never achieve. Jesus spoke about such a contrast even when he sent out the twelve to do the mission tour of the villages of Israel. [120] A "soulish" life means the suppression of the very spirit that was born again. The spirit side of us which would lead to holiness becomes suppressed and eventually closed reverting to something akin to our former state. This is a sad and desperate situation yet sadly some churches celebrate such an "achievement" and only see the "older" ways as being like the dark ages. Such churches construct a set of positive terms for such apparent advancement. These phrases or thought bubbles become buzz words for the energetic promotion of such "earthy" gatherings under the church umbrella.

When we no longer hear the voice of God what does a church on its own now do? A common approach is to fill our frantic lives with more activity to prove our worth as good church people. The situation is worse when we become full time church workers, leaders or missionaries. We could even dig into alternative modes of spirituality because they offer a chance to discover what seems to be hidden from our eyes. Frequently these mysterious ways are not biblical and head off onto sidetracks that take us further from Christ and his word but somehow make us feel more "spiritual" so they must be ok. These two methods of

---

[120] Matthew 10:39 Whoever finds their life will lose it, and whoever loses their life for my sake will find it.

coping as "churches without the Spirit" are very common and easy to fall into.

So how do we live out this prayer of Paul in our key verse?

1. We are called to a life of self denial in order to hear the Spirit through the Word of God in our spirit.
2. We must confess our pride and need to be constantly affirmed and become obedient to the Word.
3. We must lay aside our own understanding, our need to solve things and know all about what is happening and trust in the God who is always wise and infinitely knowledgeable.[121]
4. We must be honest and recognise that we have avoided the deep inner chat as to why we have no peace, no real rest, no joy.
5. We are called to worship Christ all the time, to seek his face, to live out of his righteousness. We do not need to establish our own as his is sufficient.
6. We need the daily filling of the Spirit, of the oil in our lamps, lit by faith, for the light of Christ to shine. Hallelujah.

To finish please carefully read another quote from "Hidden Treasures";
The intention is that our spirit is to be made alive so that God can speak to us; we should live for Him and for the heavenly things. Then we find rest for our souls. The heavenly things are eternal and unchangeable. When we live before God's face, we are free from people and the unrest that comes from living before their face.[122]

He will keep us until his return as he is faithful and he will do it!

---

[121] Proverbs 3:5,6
[122] This is an edited version of an article that was first published in Norwegian under the title "Pierces and divides soul from spirit" in BCC's periodical Skjulte Skatter (Hidden Treasures) in August 1955.

The Church is made up of born again believers who are led by the Holy Spirit through their revitalised human spirits. We can now worship as a body according to the truth revealed in Scripture and have the life that Christ intends. Our souls can now be directed along holy lines and our bodies can be a living sacrifice which is our divinely ordained means of worship.

www.ingramcontent.com/pod-product-compliance
Lightning Source LLC
LaVergne TN
LVHW051557070426
835507LV00021B/2620